Cram101 Textbook Outlines to accompany:

Business Communication at Work

Satterwhite and Olson-Sutton, 2nd Edition

An Academic Internet Publishers (AIPI) publication (c) 2007.

You have a discounted membership at www.Cram101.com with this book.

Get all of the practice tests for the chapters of this textbook, and access in-depth reference material for writing essays and papers. Here is an example from a Cram101 Biology text:

When you need problem solving help with math, stats, and other disciplines, www.Cram101.com will walk through the formulas and solutions step by step.

With Cram101.com online, you also have access to extensive reference material.

You will nail those essays and papers. Here is an example from a Cram101 Biology text:

Exploring Concepts

The abdominal aorta travels down the posterior wall of the abdomen, the abdominal aorta runs on the left of the inferior vena cava, giving off major blood vessels to the gut organs and kidneys. There are many recognized variants in the vasculature of the gastrointestinal system. The most common arrangement is for the abdominal aorta is to give off (in order) a

Click to Enlarge

-- celiac artery,
-- superior mesenteric artery and
-- inferior mesenteric artery.

The renal arteries usually branch from the abdominal aorta in between the celiac artery and the superior mesenteric artery.

Source: This article is licensed under the GNU Free Documentation License

Back | Close

Visit **www.Cram101.com**, click Sign Up at the top of the screen, and enter DK73DW in the promo code box on the registration screen. Access to www.Cram101.com is normally $9.95, but because you have purchased this book, your access fee is only $4.95. Sign up and stop highlighting textbooks forever.

Learning System

Cram101 Textbook Outlines is a learning system. The notes in this book are the highlights of your textbook, you will never have to highlight a book again.

How to use this book. Take this book to class, it is your notebook for the lecture. The notes and highlights on the left hand side of the pages follow the outline and order of the textbook. All you have to do is follow along while your intructor presents the lecture. Circle the items emphasized in class and add other important information on the right side. With Cram101 Textbook Outlines you'll spend less time writing and more time listening. Learning becomes more efficient.

Cram101.com Online

Increase your studying efficiency by using Cram101.com's practice tests and online reference material. It is the perfect complement to Cram101 Textbook Outlines. Use self-teaching matching tests or simulate in-class testing with comprehensive multiple choice tests, or simply use Cram's true and false tests for quick review. Cram101.com even allows you to enter your in-class notes for an integrated studying format combining the textbook notes with your class notes.

Visit **www.Cram101.com**, click Sign Up at the top of the screen, and enter **DK73DW499** in the promo code box on the registration screen. Access to www.Cram101.com is normally $9.95, but because you have purchased this book, your access fee is only $4.95. Sign up and stop highlighting textbooks forever.

Business Communication at Work
Satterwhite and Olson-Sutton, 2nd

CONTENTS

Ford	Ford is an American company that manufactures and sells automobiles worldwide. Ford introduced methods for large-scale manufacturing of cars, and large-scale management of an industrial workforce, especially elaborately engineered manufacturing sequences typified by the moving assembly lines.
Advertisement	Advertisement is the promotion of goods, services, companies and ideas, usually by an identified sponsor. Marketers see advertising as part of an overall promotional strategy.
Applicant	In many tribunal and administrative law suits, the person who initiates the claim is called the applicant.
Supervisor	A Supervisor is an employee of an organization with some of the powers and responsibilities of management, occupying a role between true manager and a regular employee. A Supervisor position is typically the first step towards being promoted into a management role.
Effective communication	When the intended meaning equals the perceived meaning it is called effective communication.
Case study	A case study is a particular method of qualitative research. Rather than using large samples and following a rigid protocol to examine a limited number of variables, case study methods involve an in-depth, longitudinal examination of a single instance or event: a case. They provide a systematic way of looking at events, collecting data, analyzing information, and reporting the results.
Supply	Supply is the aggregate amount of any material good that can be called into being at a certain price point; it comprises one half of the equation of supply and demand. In classical economic theory, a curve representing supply is one of the factors that produce price.
Trust	An arrangement in which shareholders of independent firms agree to give up their stock in exchange for trust certificates that entitle them to a share of the trust's common profits.
Goodwill	Goodwill is an important accounting concept that describes the value of a business entity not directly attributable to its tangible assets and liabilities.
Loyalty	Marketers tend to define customer loyalty as making repeat purchases. Some argue that it should be defined attitudinally as a strongly positive feeling about the brand.
Operation	A standardized method or technique that is performed repetitively, often on different materials resulting in different finished goods is called an operation.
Business operations	Business operations are those activities involved in the running of a business for the purpose of producing value for the stakeholders. The outcome of business operations is the harvesting of value from assets owned by a business.
Technology	The body of knowledge and techniques that can be used to combine economic resources to produce goods and services is called technology.
Electronic mail	Electronic mail refers to electronic written communication between individuals using computers connected to the Internet.
International Business	International business refers to any firm that engages in international trade or investment.
Jargon	Jargon is terminology, much like slang, that relates to a specific activity, profession, or group. It develops as a kind of shorthand, to express ideas that are frequently discussed between members of a group, and can also have the effect of distinguishing those belonging to a group from those who are
Management	Management characterizes the process of leading and directing all or part of an organization, often a business, through the deployment and manipulation of resources. Early twentieth-century management writer Mary Parker Follett defined management as "the art of getting things done through people."
Total quality management	The broad set of management and control processes designed to focus an entire organization and all of its employees on providing products or services that do the best possible job of satisfying the

Go to **Cram101.com** for the Practice Tests for this Chapter.

customer is called total quality management.

Continuous improvement	The constant effort to eliminate waste, reduce response time, simplify the design of both products and processes, and improve quality and customer service is referred to as continuous improvement.
Quality management	Quality management is a method for ensuring that all the activities necessary to design, develop and implement a product or service are effective and efficient with respect to the system and its performance.
Writ	Writ refers to a commandment of a court given for the purpose of compelling certain action from the defendant, and usually executed by a sheriff or other judicial officer.
Leadership	Management merely consists of leadership applied to business situations; or in other words: management forms a sub-set of the broader process of leadership.
Exchange	The trade of things of value between buyer and seller so that each is better off after the trade is called the exchange.
Contract	A contract is a "promise" or an "agreement" that is enforced or recognized by the law. In the civil law, a contract is considered to be part of the general law of obligations.
Service	Service refers to a "non tangible product" that is not embodied in a physical good and that typically effects some change in another product, person, or institution. Contrasts with good.
Distribution	Distribution in economics, the manner in which total output and income is distributed among individuals or factors.
Points	Loan origination fees that may be deductible as interest by a buyer of property. A seller of property who pays points reduces the selling price by the amount of the points paid for the buyer.
Draft	A signed, written order by which one party instructs another party to pay a specified sum to a third party, at sight or at a specific date is a draft.
Receiver	A person that is appointed as a custodian of other people's property by a court of law or a creditor of the owner, pending a lawsuit or reorganization is called a receiver.
Aid	Assistance provided by countries and by international institutions such as the World Bank to developing countries in the form of monetary grants, loans at low interest rates, in kind, or a combination of these is called aid. Aid can also refer to assistance of any type rendered to benefit some group or individual.
Balance	In banking and accountancy, the outstanding balance is the amount of money owned, (or due), that remains in a deposit account (or a loan account) at a given date, after all past remittances, payments and withdrawal have been accounted for. It can be positive (then, in the balance sheet of a firm, it is an asset) or negative (a liability).
Commodity	Could refer to any good, but in trade a commodity is usually a raw material or primary product that enters into international trade, such as metals or basic agricultural products.
Composition	An out-of-court settlement in which creditors agree to accept a fractional settlement on their original claim is referred to as composition.
Interest	In finance and economics, interest is the price paid by a borrower for the use of a lender's money. In other words, interest is the amount of paid to "rent" money for a period of time.
Accounting	A system that collects and processes financial information about an organization and reports that information to decision makers is referred to as accounting.
Personnel	A collective term for all of the employees of an organization. Personnel is also commonly used to refer to the personnel management function or the organizational unit responsible for administering personnel programs.

Expense	In accounting, an expense represents an event in which an asset is used up or a liability is incurred. In terms of the accounting equation, expenses reduce owners' equity.
Confirmed	When the seller's bank agrees to assume liability on the letter of credit issued by the buyer's bank the transaction is confirmed. The term means that the credit is not only backed up by the issuing foreign bank, but that payment is also guaranteed by the notifying American bank.
Alignment	Term that refers to optimal coordination among disparate departments and divisions within a firm is referred to as alignment.
Browser	A program that allows a user to connect to the World Wide Web by simply typing in a URL is a browser.

Composition	An out-of-court settlement in which creditors agree to accept a fractional settlement on their original claim is referred to as composition.
Interest	In finance and economics, interest is the price paid by a borrower for the use of a lender's money. In other words, interest is the amount of paid to "rent" money for a period of time.
Argument	The discussion by counsel for the respective parties of their contentions on the law and the facts of the case being tried in order to aid the jury in arriving at a correct and just conclusion is called argument.
Writ	Writ refers to a commandment of a court given for the purpose of compelling certain action from the defendant, and usually executed by a sheriff or other judicial officer.
Comprehensive	A comprehensive refers to a layout accurate in size, color, scheme, and other necessary details to show how a final ad will look. For presentation only, never for reproduction.
Option	A contract that gives the purchaser the option to buy or sell the underlying financial instrument at a specified price, called the exercise price or strike price, within a specific period of time.
Receiver	A person that is appointed as a custodian of other people's property by a court of law or a creditor of the owner, pending a lawsuit or reorganization is called a receiver.
Consideration	Consideration in contract law, a basic requirement for an enforceable agreement under traditional contract principles, defined in this text as legal value, bargained for and given in exchange for an act or promise. In corporation law, cash or property contributed to a corporation in exchange for shares, or a promise to contribute such cash or property.
Realization	Realization is the sale of assets when an entity is being liquidated.
Trend	Trend refers to the long-term movement of an economic variable, such as its average rate of increase or decrease over enough years to encompass several business cycles.
Advertisement	Advertisement is the promotion of goods, services, companies and ideas, usually by an identified sponsor. Marketers see advertising as part of an overall promotional strategy.
Remainder	A remainder in property law is a future interest created in a transferee that is capable of becoming possessory upon the natural termination of a prior estate created by the same instrument.
Jargon	Jargon is terminology, much like slang, that relates to a specific activity, profession, or group. It develops as a kind of shorthand, to express ideas that are frequently discussed between members of a group, and can also have the effect of distinguishing those belonging to a group from those who are not.
Specialist	A specialist is a trader who makes a market in one or several stocks and holds the limit order book for those stocks.
Evaluation	The consumer's appraisal of the product or brand on important attributes is called evaluation.
Hearing	A hearing is a proceeding before a court or other decision-making body or officer. A hearing is generally distinguished from a trial in that it is usually shorter and often less formal.
Holding	The holding is a court's determination of a matter of law based on the issue presented in the particular case. In other words: under this law, with these facts, this result.
Supply	Supply is the aggregate amount of any material good that can be called into being at a certain price point; it comprises one half of the equation of supply and demand. In classical economic theory, a curve representing supply is one of the factors that produce price.
Context	The effect of the background under which a message often takes on more and richer meaning is

Go to **Cram101.com** for the Practice Tests for this Chapter.

	a context. Context is especially important in cross-cultural interactions because some cultures are said to be high context or low context.
Service	Service refers to a "non tangible product" that is not embodied in a physical good and that typically effects some change in another product, person, or institution. Contrasts with good.
Advertising	Advertising refers to paid, nonpersonal communication through various media by organizations and individuals who are in some way identified in the advertising message.
Forming	The first stage of team development, where the team is formed and the objectives for the team are set is referred to as forming.
Property	Assets defined in the broadest legal sense. Property includes the unrealized receivables of a cash basis taxpayer, but not services rendered.

101

11

Preparation	Preparation refers to usually the first stage in the creative process. It includes education and formal training.
Budget	Budget refers to an account, usually for a year, of the planned expenditures and the expected receipts of an entity. For a government, the receipts are tax revenues.
Supply	Supply is the aggregate amount of any material good that can be called into being at a certain price point; it comprises one half of the equation of supply and demand. In classical economic theory, a curve representing supply is one of the factors that produce price.
Manufacturing	Production of goods primarily by the application of labor and capital to raw materials and other intermediate inputs, in contrast to agriculture, mining, forestry, fishing, and services a manufacturing.
Productivity	Productivity refers to the total output of goods and services in a given period of time divided by work hours.
Draft	A signed, written order by which one party instructs another party to pay a specified sum to a third party, at sight or at a specific date is a draft.
Effective communication	When the intended meaning equals the perceived meaning it is called effective communication.
Principal	In agency law, one under whose direction an agent acts and for whose benefit that agent acts is a principal.
Credibility	The extent to which a source is perceived as having knowledge, skill, or experience relevant to a communication topic and can be trusted to give an unbiased opinion or present objective information on the issue is called credibility.
Service	Service refers to a "non tangible product" that is not embodied in a physical good and that typically effects some change in another product, person, or institution. Contrasts with good.
Annual report	An annual report is prepared by corporate management that presents financial information including financial statements, footnotes, and the management discussion and analysis.
Standing	Standing refers to the legal requirement that anyone seeking to challenge a particular action in court must demonstrate that such action substantially affects his legitimate interests before he will be entitled to bring suit.
Investment	Investment refers to spending for the production and accumulation of capital and additions to inventories. In a financial sense, buying an asset with the expectation of making a return.
Closing	The finalization of a real estate sales transaction that passes title to the property from the seller to the buyer is referred to as a closing. Closing is a sales term which refers to the process of making a sale. It refers to reaching the final step, which may be an exchange of money or acquiring a signature.
Insurance	Insurance refers to a system by which individuals can reduce their exposure to risk of large losses by spreading the risks among a large number of persons.
Pledge	In law a pledge (also pawn) is a bailment of personal property as a security for some debt or engagement.
Policy	Similar to a script in that a policy can be a less than completely rational decision-making method. Involves the use of a pre-existing set of decision steps for any problem that presents itself.
Receiver	A person that is appointed as a custodian of other people's property by a court of law or a creditor of the owner, pending a lawsuit or reorganization is called a receiver.

Go to **Cram101.com** for the Practice Tests for this Chapter.

Users	Users refer to people in the organization who actually use the product or service purchased by the buying center.
Technology	The body of knowledge and techniques that can be used to combine economic resources to produce goods and services is called technology.
Leadership	Management merely consists of leadership applied to business situations; or in other words: management forms a sub-set of the broader process of leadership.
Trademark	A distinctive word, name, symbol, device, or combination thereof, which enables consumers to identify favored products or services and which may find protection under state or federal law is a trademark.
Interest	In finance and economics, interest is the price paid by a borrower for the use of a lender's money. In other words, interest is the amount of paid to "rent" money for a period of time.
Option	A contract that gives the purchaser the option to buy or sell the underlying financial instrument at a specified price, called the exercise price or strike price, within a specific period of time.
Supervisor	A Supervisor is an employee of an organization with some of the powers and responsibilities of management, occupying a role between true manager and a regular employee. A Supervisor position is typically the first step towards being promoted into a management role.
Promotion	Promotion refers to all the techniques sellers use to motivate people to buy products or services. An attempt by marketers to inform people about products and to persuade them to participate in an exchange.
Fund	Independent accounting entity with a self-balancing set of accounts segregated for the purposes of carrying on specific activities is referred to as a fund.
Expense	In accounting, an expense represents an event in which an asset is used up or a liability is incurred. In terms of the accounting equation, expenses reduce owners' equity.
Personnel	A collective term for all of the employees of an organization. Personnel is also commonly used to refer to the personnel management function or the organizational unit responsible for administering personnel programs.
Layoff	A layoff is the termination of an employee or (more commonly) a group of employees for business reasons, such as the decision that certain positions are no longer necessary.
Consideration	Consideration in contract law, a basic requirement for an enforceable agreement under traditional contract principles, defined in this text as legal value, bargained for and given in exchange for an act or promise. In corporation law, cash or property contributed to a corporation in exchange for shares, or a promise to contribute such cash or property.
Verification	Verification refers to the final stage of the creative process where the validity or truthfulness of the insight is determined. The feedback portion of communication in which the receiver sends a message to the source indicating receipt of the message and the degree to which he or she understood the message.
Sole proprietorship	A sole proprietorship is a business which legally has no separate existence from its owner. Hence, the limitations of liability enjoyed by a corporation do not apply.
Asset	An item of property, such as land, capital, money, a share in ownership, or a claim on others for future payment, such as a bond or a bank deposit is an asset.
Agent	A person who makes economic decisions for another economic actor. A hired manager operates as an agent for a firm's owner.
Estate	An estate is the totality of the legal rights, interests, entitlements and obligations

Go to **Cram101.com** for the Practice Tests for this Chapter.

	attaching to property. In the context of wills and probate, it refers to the totality of the property which the deceased owned or in which some interest was held.
Environmental protection agency	An administrative agency created by Congress in 1970 to coordinate the implementation and enforcement of the federal environmental protection laws is referred to as the Environmental Protection Agency or EPA.
Liability	A liability is a present obligation of the enterprise arizing from past events, the settlement of which is expected to result in an outflow from the enterprise of resources embodying economic benefits.
Brief	Brief refers to a statement of a party's case or legal arguments, usually prepared by an attorney. Also used to make legal arguments before appellate courts.
Portfolio	In finance, a portfolio is a collection of investments held by an institution or a private individual. Holding but not always a portfolio is part of an investment and risk-limiting strategy called diversification. By owning several assets, certain types of risk (in particular specific risk) can be reduced.

Go to **Cram101.com** for the Practice Tests for this Chapter.

Prejudice	Prejudice is, as the name implies, the process of "pre-judging" something. It implies coming to a judgment on a subject before learning where the preponderance of evidence actually lies, or forming a judgment without direct experience.
Interest	In finance and economics, interest is the price paid by a borrower for the use of a lender's money. In other words, interest is the amount of paid to "rent" money for a period of time.
Market	A market is, as defined in economics, a social arrangement that allows buyers and sellers to discover information and carry out a voluntary exchange of goods or services.
Gain	In finance, gain is a profit or an increase in value of an investment such as a stock or bond. Gain is calculated by fair market value or the proceeds from the sale of the investment minus the sum of the purchase price and all costs associated with it.
Receiver	A person that is appointed as a custodian of other people's property by a court of law or a creditor of the owner, pending a lawsuit or reorganization is called a receiver.
Teamwork	That which occurs when group members work together in ways that utilize their skills well to accomplish a purpose is called teamwork.
Active listening	Active listening is a way of "listening for meaning" in which the listener checks with the speaker to see that a statement has been correctly heard and understood. The goal of active listening is to improve mutual understanding.
Hearing	A hearing is a proceeding before a court or other decision-making body or officer. A hearing is generally distinguished from a trial in that it is usually shorter and often less formal.
Points	Loan origination fees that may be deductible as interest by a buyer of property. A seller of property who pays points reduces the selling price by the amount of the points paid for the buyer.
Expense	In accounting, an expense represents an event in which an asset is used up or a liability is incurred. In terms of the accounting equation, expenses reduce owners' equity.
Body language	Body language is a broad term for forms of communication using body movements or gestures instead of, or in addition to, sounds, verbal language, or other forms of communication.
Supervisor	A Supervisor is an employee of an organization with some of the powers and responsibilities of management, occupying a role between true manager and a regular employee. A Supervisor position is typically the first step towards being promoted into a management role.
Negligence	The omission to do something that a reasonable person, guided by those considerations that ordinarily regulate human affairs, would do, or doing something that a prudent and reasonable person would not do is negligence.
Nonverbal communication	The many additional ways that communication is accomplished beyond the oral or written word is referred to as nonverbal communication.
Discount	The difference between the face value of a bond and its selling price, when a bond is sold for less than its face value it's referred to as a discount.
International trade	The export of goods and services from a country and the import of goods and services into a country is referred to as the international trade.
Gap	In December of 1995, Gap became the first major North American retailer to accept independent monitoring of the working conditions in a contract factory producing its garments. Gap is the largest specialty retailer in the United States.
Closing	The finalization of a real estate sales transaction that passes title to the property from the seller to the buyer is referred to as a closing. Closing is a sales term which refers to the process of making a sale. It refers to reaching the final step, which may be an exchange

Go to **Cram101.com** for the Practice Tests for this Chapter.

of money or acquiring a signature.

Trust

An arrangement in which shareholders of independent firms agree to give up their stock in exchange for trust certificates that entitle them to a share of the trust's common profits.

Mistake

In contract law a mistake is incorrect understanding by one or more parties to a contract and may be used as grounds to invalidate the agreement. Common law has identified three different types of mistake in contract: unilateral mistake, mutual mistake, and common mistake.

Nonverbal communication	The many additional ways that communication is accomplished beyond the oral or written word is referred to as nonverbal communication.
Receiver	A person that is appointed as a custodian of other people's property by a court of law or a creditor of the owner, pending a lawsuit or reorganization is called a receiver.
Management	Management characterizes the process of leading and directing all or part of an organization, often a business, through the deployment and manipulation of resources. Early twentieth-century management writer Mary Parker Follett defined management as "the art of getting things done through people."
Time management	Time Management refers to tools or techniques for planning and scheduling time, usually with the aim to increase the effectiveness and/or efficiency of personal and corporate time use.
Technology	The body of knowledge and techniques that can be used to combine economic resources to produce goods and services is called technology.
Preparation	Preparation refers to usually the first stage in the creative process. It includes education and formal training.
Policy	Similar to a script in that a policy can be a less than completely rational decision-making method. Involves the use of a pre-existing set of decision steps for any problem that presents itself.
Effective communication	When the intended meaning equals the perceived meaning it is called effective communication.
Drucker	Drucker as a business thinker took off in the 1940s, when his initial writings on politics and society won him access to the internal workings of General Motors, which was one of the largest companies in the world at that time. His experiences in Europe had left him fascinated with the problem of authority.
Interest	In finance and economics, interest is the price paid by a borrower for the use of a lender's money. In other words, interest is the amount of paid to "rent" money for a period of time.
Appreciation	Appreciation refers to a rise in the value of a country's currency on the exchange market, relative either to a particular other currency or to a weighted average of other currencies. The currency is said to appreciate. Opposite of 'depreciation.' Appreciation can also refer to the increase in value of any asset.
Closing	The finalization of a real estate sales transaction that passes title to the property from the seller to the buyer is referred to as a closing. Closing is a sales term which refers to the process of making a sale. It refers to reaching the final step, which may be an exchange of money or acquiring a signature.
Service	Service refers to a "non tangible product" that is not embodied in a physical good and that typically effects some change in another product, person, or institution. Contrasts with good.
Warranty	An obligation of a company to replace defective goods or correct any deficiencies in performance or quality of a product is called a warranty.
Remainder	A remainder in property law is a future interest created in a transferee that is capable of becoming possessory upon the natural termination of a prior estate created by the same instrument.
Equity	Equity is the name given to the set of legal principles, in countries following the English common law tradition, which supplement strict rules of law where their application would operate harshly, so as to achieve what is sometimes referred to as "natural justice."
Interest rate	The rate of return on bonds, loans, or deposits. When one speaks of 'the' interest rate, it

is usually in a model where there is only one.

Forming	The first stage of team development, where the team is formed and the objectives for the team are set is referred to as forming.
Bond	Bond refers to a debt instrument, issued by a borrower and promising a specified stream of payments to the purchaser, usually regular interest payments plus a final repayment of principal.
Credit	Credit refers to a recording as positive in the balance of payments, any transaction that gives rise to a payment into the country, such as an export, the sale of an asset, or borrowing from abroad.
Conversion	Conversion refers to any distinct act of dominion wrongfully exerted over another's personal property in denial of or inconsistent with his rights therein. That tort committed by a person who deals with chattels not belonging to him in a manner that is inconsistent with the ownership of the lawful owner.
Consideration	Consideration in contract law, a basic requirement for an enforceable agreement under traditional contract principles, defined in this text as legal value, bargained for and given in exchange for an act or promise. In corporation law, cash or property contributed to a corporation in exchange for shares, or a promise to contribute such cash or property.
Complete information	Complete information refers to the assumption that economic agents know everything that they need to know in order to make optimal decisions. Types of incomplete information are uncertainty and asymmetric information.
Foundation	A Foundation is a type of philanthropic organization set up by either individuals or institutions as a legal entity (either as a corporation or trust) with the purpose of distributing grants to support causes in line with the goals of the foundation.
Mortgage	Mortgage refers to a note payable issued for property, such as a house, usually repaid in equal installments consisting of part principle and part interest, over a specified period.
Mortgage company	Mortgage company refers to a financial institution that lends money to borrowers to purchase property.
Advertising	Advertising refers to paid, nonpersonal communication through various media by organizations and individuals who are in some way identified in the advertising message.
Copywriter	Individual who helps conceive the ideas for ads and commercials and writes the words or copy for them is referred to as copywriter.
Brief	Brief refers to a statement of a party's case or legal arguments, usually prepared by an attorney. Also used to make legal arguments before appellate courts.
Writ	Writ refers to a commandment of a court given for the purpose of compelling certain action from the defendant, and usually executed by a sheriff or other judicial officer.
Gain	In finance, gain is a profit or an increase in value of an investment such as a stock or bond. Gain is calculated by fair market value or the proceeds from the sale of the investment minus the sum of the purchase price and all costs associated with it.
Brainstorming	Brainstorming refers to a technique designed to overcome our natural tendency to evaluate and criticize ideas and thereby reduce the creative output of those ideas. People are encouraged to produce ideas/options without criticizing, often at a very fast pace to minimize our natural tendency to criticize.
Draft	A signed, written order by which one party instructs another party to pay a specified sum to a third party, at sight or at a specific date is a draft.

Go to **Cram101.com** for the Practice Tests for this Chapter.

Goodwill	Goodwill is an important accounting concept that describes the value of a business entity not directly attributable to its tangible assets and liabilities.
Bleed	Printed matter that runs over the edges of an outdoor board or of a page, leaving no margin is called a bleed.
Mistake	In contract law a mistake is incorrect understanding by one or more parties to a contract and may be used as grounds to invalidate the agreement. Common law has identified three different types of mistake in contract: unilateral mistake, mutual mistake, and common mistake.
Insurance	Insurance refers to a system by which individuals can reduce their exposure to risk of large losses by spreading the risks among a large number of persons.
Investment	Investment refers to spending for the production and accumulation of capital and additions to inventories. In a financial sense, buying an asset with the expectation of making a return.
Applicant	In many tribunal and administrative law suits, the person who initiates the claim is called the applicant.
Promotion	Promotion refers to all the techniques sellers use to motivate people to buy products or services. An attempt by marketers to inform people about products and to persuade them to participate in an exchange.
Human resources	Human resources refers to the individuals within the firm, and to the portion of the firm's organization that deals with hiring, firing, training, and other personnel issues.
Product line	A group of products that are physically similar or are intended for a similar market are called the product line.
Standing	Standing refers to the legal requirement that anyone seeking to challenge a particular action in court must demonstrate that such action substantially affects his legitimate interests before he will be entitled to bring suit.
Compromise	Compromise occurs when the interaction is moderately important to meeting goals and the goals are neither completely compatible nor completely incompatible.
Committee	A long-lasting, sometimes permanent team in the organization structure created to deal with tasks that recur regularly is the committee.
Corporation	A legal entity chartered by a state or the Federal government that is distinct and separate from the individuals who own it is a corporation. This separation gives the corporation unique powers which other legal entities lack.
Manufacturing	Production of goods primarily by the application of labor and capital to raw materials and other intermediate inputs, in contrast to agriculture, mining, forestry, fishing, and services a manufacturing.
Regulation	Regulation refers to restrictions state and federal laws place on business with regard to the conduct of its activities.

Brainstorming	Brainstorming refers to a technique designed to overcome our natural tendency to evaluate and criticize ideas and thereby reduce the creative output of those ideas. People are encouraged to produce ideas/options without criticizing, often at a very fast pace to minimize our natural tendency to criticize.
Points	Loan origination fees that may be deductible as interest by a buyer of property. A seller of property who pays points reduces the selling price by the amount of the points paid for the buyer.
Comprehensive	A comprehensive refers to a layout accurate in size, color, scheme, and other necessary details to show how a final ad will look. For presentation only, never for reproduction.
Core	A core is the set of feasible allocations in an economy that cannot be improved upon by subset of the set of the economy's consumers (a coalition). In construction, when the force in an element is within a certain center section, the core, the element will only be under compression.
Interest	In finance and economics, interest is the price paid by a borrower for the use of a lender's money. In other words, interest is the amount of paid to "rent" money for a period of time.
Appeal	Appeal refers to the act of asking an appellate court to overturn a decision after the trial court's final judgment has been entered.
Technology	The body of knowledge and techniques that can be used to combine economic resources to produce goods and services is called technology.
Market	A market is, as defined in economics, a social arrangement that allows buyers and sellers to discover information and carry out a voluntary exchange of goods or services.
Merchant	Under the Uniform Commercial Code, one who regularly deals in goods of the kind sold in the contract at issue, or holds himself out as having special knowledge or skill relevant to such goods, or who makes the sale through an agent who regularly deals in such goods or claims such knowledge or skill is referred to as merchant.
Burroughs	Burroughs developed three highly innovative architectures, based on the design philosophy of "language directed design". Their machine instruction sets favored one or many high level programming languages, such as ALGOL, COBOL or FORTRAN. All three architectures were considered "main-frame" class machines.
Inventory	Tangible property held for sale in the normal course of business or used in producing goods or services for sale is an inventory.
Warehouse	Warehouse refers to a location, often decentralized, that a firm uses to store, consolidate, age, or mix stock; house product-recall programs; or ease tax burdens.
Analyst	Analyst refers to a person or tool with a primary function of information analysis, generally with a more limited, practical and short term set of goals than a researcher.
Operation	A standardized method or technique that is performed repetitively, often on different materials resulting in different finished goods is called an operation.
Integration	Economic integration refers to reducing barriers among countries to transactions and to movements of goods, capital, and labor, including harmonization of laws, regulations, and standards. Integrated markets theoretically function as a unified market.
Global web	When different stages of value chain are dispersed to those locations around the globe where value added is maximized or where costs of value creation are minimized, we have global web.
Wireless communication	Wireless communication refers to a method of communication that uses low-powered radio waves to transmit data between devices. The term refers to communication without cables or cords, chiefly using radio frequency and infrared waves. Common uses include the various

	communications defined by the IrDA, the wireless networking of computers and cellular mobile phones.
Option	A contract that gives the purchaser the option to buy or sell the underlying financial instrument at a specified price, called the exercise price or strike price, within a specific period of time.
Contract	A contract is a "promise" or an "agreement" that is enforced or recognized by the law. In the civil law, a contract is considered to be part of the general law of obligations.
Firm	An organization that employs resources to produce a good or service for profit and owns and operates one or more plants is referred to as a firm.
Cabinet	The heads of the executive departments of a jurisdiction who report to and advise its chief executive; examples would include the president's cabinet, the governor's cabinet, and the mayor's cabinet.
Browser	A program that allows a user to connect to the World Wide Web by simply typing in a URL is a browser.
Management	Management characterizes the process of leading and directing all or part of an organization, often a business, through the deployment and manipulation of resources. Early twentieth-century management writer Mary Parker Follett defined management as "the art of getting things done through people."
Estate	An estate is the totality of the legal rights, interests, entitlements and obligations attaching to property. In the context of wills and probate, it refers to the totality of the property which the deceased owned or in which some interest was held.
Agent	A person who makes economic decisions for another economic actor. A hired manager operates as an agent for a firm's owner.
Property	Assets defined in the broadest legal sense. Property includes the unrealized receivables of a cash basis taxpayer, but not services rendered.
Incorporation	Incorporation is the forming of a new corporation. The corporation may be a business, a non-profit organization or even a government of a new city or town.
Production	The creation of finished goods and services using the factors of production: land, labor, capital, entrepreneurship, and knowledge.
Marketing	Promoting and selling products or services to customers, or prospective customers, is referred to as marketing.
Promotion	Promotion refers to all the techniques sellers use to motivate people to buy products or services. An attempt by marketers to inform people about products and to persuade them to participate in an exchange.
Service	Service refers to a "non tangible product" that is not embodied in a physical good and that typically effects some change in another product, person, or institution. Contrasts with good.
Commercial online services	Companies that provide electronic information and marketing services to subscribers who are charged a monthly fee are referred to as commercial online services.
Inception	The date and time on which coverage under an insurance policy takes effect is inception. Also refers to the date at which a stock or mutual fund was first traded.
Configuration	An organization's shape, which reflects the division of labor and the means of coordinating the divided tasks is configuration.
Administrator	Administrator refers to the personal representative appointed by a probate court to settle

the estate of a deceased person who died.

Policy	Similar to a script in that a policy can be a less than completely rational decision-making method. Involves the use of a pre-existing set of decision steps for any problem that presents itself.
Effective communication	When the intended meaning equals the perceived meaning it is called effective communication.
Exchange	The trade of things of value between buyer and seller so that each is better off after the trade is called the exchange.
Users	Users refer to people in the organization who actually use the product or service purchased by the buying center.
Attachment	Attachment in general, the process of taking a person's property under an appropriate judicial order by an appropriate officer of the court. Used for a variety of purposes, including the acquisition of jurisdiction over the property seized and the securing of property that may be used to satisfy a debt.
Default	In finance, default occurs when a debtor has not met its legal obligations according to the debt contract, e.g. it has not made a scheduled payment, or violated a covenant (condition) of the debt contract.
Microsoft	Microsoft is a multinational computer technology corporation with 2004 global annual sales of US$39.79 billion and 71,553 employees in 102 countries and regions as of July 2006. It develops, manufactures, licenses, and supports a wide range of software products for computing devices.
Termination	The ending of a corporation that occurs only after the winding-up of the corporation's affairs, the liquidation of its assets, and the distribution of the proceeds to the claimants are referred to as a termination.
License	A license in the sphere of Intellectual Property Rights (IPR) is a document, contract or agreement giving permission or the 'right' to a legally-definable entity to do something (such as manufacture a product or to use a service), or to apply something (such as a trademark), with the objective of achieving commercial gain.
Wholesale	According to the United Nations Statistics Division Wholesale is the resale of new and used goods to retailers, to industrial, commercial, institutional or professional users, or to other wholesalers, or involves acting as an agent or broker in buying merchandise for, or selling merchandise, to such persons or companies.
Aid	Assistance provided by countries and by international institutions such as the World Bank to developing countries in the form of monetary grants, loans at low interest rates, in kind, or a combination of these is called aid. Aid can also refer to assistance of any type rendered to benefit some group or individual.
Personnel	A collective term for all of the employees of an organization. Personnel is also commonly used to refer to the personnel management function or the organizational unit responsible for administering personnel programs.
Receiver	A person that is appointed as a custodian of other people's property by a court of law or a creditor of the owner, pending a lawsuit or reorganization is called a receiver.
Draft	A signed, written order by which one party instructs another party to pay a specified sum to a third party, at sight or at a specific date is a draft.
Project management	Project management software is a term covering many types of software, including scheduling, resource allocation, collaboration software, communication and documentation systems, which

Go to **Cram101.com** for the Practice Tests for this Chapter.

software	are used to deal with the complexity of large projects.
Project management	Project management is the discipline of organizing and managing resources in such a way that these resources deliver all the work required to complete a project within defined scope, time, and cost constraints.
Ergonomics	Ergonomics refers to the interface between individuals' physiological characteristics and the physical work environment.
Credit union	A credit union is a not-for-profit co-operative financial institution that is owned and controlled by its members, through the election of a volunteer Board of Directors elected from the membership itself.
Credit	Credit refers to a recording as positive in the balance of payments, any transaction that gives rise to a payment into the country, such as an export, the sale of an asset, or borrowing from abroad.
Union	A worker association that bargains with employers over wages and working conditions is called a union.

Draft	A signed, written order by which one party instructs another party to pay a specified sum to a third party, at sight or at a specific date is a draft.
Technology	The body of knowledge and techniques that can be used to combine economic resources to produce goods and services is called technology.
Advertising	Advertising refers to paid, nonpersonal communication through various media by organizations and individuals who are in some way identified in the advertising message.
Public relations	Public relations refers to the management function that evaluates public attitudes, changes policies and procedures in response to the public's requests, and executes a program of action and information to earn public understanding and acceptance.
Operation	A standardized method or technique that is performed repetitively, often on different materials resulting in different finished goods is called an operation.
Electronic mail	Electronic mail refers to electronic written communication between individuals using computers connected to the Internet.
Trend	Trend refers to the long-term movement of an economic variable, such as its average rate of increase or decrease over enough years to encompass several business cycles.
Default	In finance, default occurs when a debtor has not met its legal obligations according to the debt contract, e.g. it has not made a scheduled payment, or violated a covenant (condition) of the debt contract.
Margin	A deposit by a buyer in stocks with a seller or a stockbroker, as security to cover fluctuations in the market in reference to stocks that the buyer has purchased but for which he has not paid is a margin. Commodities are also traded on margin.
Distribution	Distribution in economics, the manner in which total output and income is distributed among individuals or factors.
Attachment	Attachment in general, the process of taking a person's property under an appropriate judicial order by an appropriate officer of the court. Used for a variety of purposes, including the acquisition of jurisdiction over the property seized and the securing of property that may be used to satisfy a debt.
Administration	Administration refers to the management and direction of the affairs of governments and institutions; a collective term for all policymaking officials of a government; the execution and implementation of public policy.
Fiscal year	A fiscal year is a 12-month period used for calculating annual ("yearly") financial reports in businesses and other organizations. In many jurisdictions, regulatory laws regarding accounting require such reports once per twelve months, but do not require that the twelve months constitute a calendar year (i.e. January to December).
Insurance	Insurance refers to a system by which individuals can reduce their exposure to risk of large losses by spreading the risks among a large number of persons.
Medicare	Medicare refers to federal program that is financed by payroll taxes and provides for compulsory hospital insurance for senior citizens and low-cost voluntary insurance to help older Americans pay physicians' fees.
Policy	Similar to a script in that a policy can be a less than completely rational decision-making method. Involves the use of a pre-existing set of decision steps for any problem that presents itself.
Option	A contract that gives the purchaser the option to buy or sell the underlying financial instrument at a specified price, called the exercise price or strike price, within a specific period of time.

Aid	Assistance provided by countries and by international institutions such as the World Bank to developing countries in the form of monetary grants, loans at low interest rates, in kind, or a combination of these is called aid. Aid can also refer to assistance of any type rendered to benefit some group or individual.
Marketing	Promoting and selling products or services to customers, or prospective customers, is referred to as marketing.
Authority	Authority in agency law, refers to an agent's ability to affect his principal's legal relations with third parties. Also used to refer to an actor's legal power or ability to do something. In addition, sometimes used to refer to a statute, case, or other legal source that justifies a particular result.
Interest	In finance and economics, interest is the price paid by a borrower for the use of a lender's money. In other words, interest is the amount of paid to "rent" money for a period of time.
Receiver	A person that is appointed as a custodian of other people's property by a court of law or a creditor of the owner, pending a lawsuit or reorganization is called a receiver.
Supply	Supply is the aggregate amount of any material good that can be called into being at a certain price point; it comprises one half of the equation of supply and demand. In classical economic theory, a curve representing supply is one of the factors that produce price.
Warrant	A warrant is a security that entitles the holder to buy or sell a certain additional quantity of an underlying security at an agreed-upon price, at the holder's discretion.
Brief	Brief refers to a statement of a party's case or legal arguments, usually prepared by an attorney. Also used to make legal arguments before appellate courts.
Property	Assets defined in the broadest legal sense. Property includes the unrealized receivables of a cash basis taxpayer, but not services rendered.
Remainder	A remainder in property law is a future interest created in a transferee that is capable of becoming possessory upon the natural termination of a prior estate created by the same instrument.
Teamwork	That which occurs when group members work together in ways that utilize their skills well to accomplish a purpose is called teamwork.
Logo	Logo refers to device or other brand name that cannot be spoken.
Closing	The finalization of a real estate sales transaction that passes title to the property from the seller to the buyer is referred to as a closing. Closing is a sales term which refers to the process of making a sale. It refers to reaching the final step, which may be an exchange of money or acquiring a signature.
Preference	The act of a debtor in paying or securing one or more of his creditors in a manner more favorable to them than to other creditors or to the exclusion of such other creditors is a preference. In the absence of statute, a preference is perfectly good, but to be legal it must be bona fide, and not a mere subterfuge of the debtor to secure a future benefit to himself or to prevent the application of his property to his debts.
Human resources	Human resources refers to the individuals within the firm, and to the portion of the firm's organization that deals with hiring, firing, training, and other personnel issues.
Administrator	Administrator refers to the personal representative appointed by a probate court to settle the estate of a deceased person who died.
Personnel	A collective term for all of the employees of an organization. Personnel is also commonly used to refer to the personnel management function or the organizational unit responsible for administering personnel programs.

Go to **Cram101.com** for the Practice Tests for this Chapter.

Postal Service	The postal service was created in Philadelphia under Benjamin Franklin on July 26, 1775 by decree of the Second Continental Congress. Based on a clause in the United States Constitution empowering Congress "To establish Post Offices and post Roads."
Service	Service refers to a "non tangible product" that is not embodied in a physical good and that typically effects some change in another product, person, or institution. Contrasts with good.
United parcel service	United Parcel Service is the world's largest package delivery company, delivering more than 14 million packages a day to more than 200 countries around the world. It has recently expanded its operations to include logistics and other transportation-related areas.
Federal Express	The company officially began operations on April 17, 1973, utilizing a network of 14 Dassault Falcon 20s which connected 25 U.S. cities. FedEx, the first cargo airline to use jet aircraft for its services, expanded greatly after the deregulation of the cargo airlines sector. Federal Express use of the hub-spoke distribution paradigm in air freight enabled it to become a world leader in its field.
Capital	Capital generally refers to financial wealth, especially that used to start or maintain a business. In classical economics, capital is one of four factors of production, the others being land and labor and entrepreneurship.
Corporation	A legal entity chartered by a state or the Federal government that is distinct and separate from the individuals who own it is a corporation. This separation gives the corporation unique powers which other legal entities lack.
Promotion	Promotion refers to all the techniques sellers use to motivate people to buy products or services. An attempt by marketers to inform people about products and to persuade them to participate in an exchange.
Sales promotion	Sales promotion refers to the promotional tool that stimulates consumer purchasing and dealer interest by means of short-term activities.
Accord	An agreement whereby the parties agree to accept something different in satisfaction of the original contract is an accord.
Production	The creation of finished goods and services using the factors of production: land, labor, capital, entrepreneurship, and knowledge.
United States Postal Service	The United States Postal Service is an "independent establishment of the executive branch" of the United States government. It is the third-largest employer in the United States (after the United States Department of Defense and Wal-Mart) and operates the largest civilian vehicle fleet in the world, with an estimated 260,000 vehicles.
Bar code	Bar code refers to a printed code that makes use of lines of various widths to encode data about products.
Invoice	The itemized bill for a transaction, stating the nature of the transaction and its cost. In international trade, the invoice price is often the preferred basis for levying an ad valorem tariff.
News release	A publicity tool consisting of an announcement regarding changes in the company or the product line is called a news release.
Audit	An examination of the financial reports to ensure that they represent what they claim and conform with generally accepted accounting principles is referred to as audit.
Management	Management characterizes the process of leading and directing all or part of an organization, often a business, through the deployment and manipulation of resources. Early twentieth-century management writer Mary Parker Follett defined management as "the art of getting

Go to **Cram101.com** for the Practice Tests for this Chapter.

Go to **Cram101.com** for the Practice Tests for this Chapter.
And, **NEVER** highlight a book again!

things done through people."

Foundation	A Foundation is a type of philanthropic organization set up by either individuals or institutions as a legal entity (either as a corporation or trust) with the purpose of distributing grants to support causes in line with the goals of the foundation.
Firm	An organization that employs resources to produce a good or service for profit and owns and operates one or more plants is referred to as a firm.

Interest	In finance and economics, interest is the price paid by a borrower for the use of a lender's money. In other words, interest is the amount of paid to "rent" money for a period of time.
Compromise	Compromise occurs when the interaction is moderately important to meeting goals and the goals are neither completely compatible nor completely incompatible.
Productivity	Productivity refers to the total output of goods and services in a given period of time divided by work hours.
Management	Management characterizes the process of leading and directing all or part of an organization, often a business, through the deployment and manipulation of resources. Early twentieth-century management writer Mary Parker Follett defined management as "the art of getting things done through people."
Smoothing	That which involves playing down differences and finding areas of agreement are referred to as accommodation or smoothing.
Conflict management	Conflict management refers to the long-term management of intractable conflicts. It is the label for the variety of ways by which people handle grievances -- standing up for what they consider to be right and against what they consider to be wrong.
Supervisor	A Supervisor is an employee of an organization with some of the powers and responsibilities of management, occupying a role between true manager and a regular employee. A Supervisor position is typically the first step towards being promoted into a management role.
Asset	An item of property, such as land, capital, money, a share in ownership, or a claim on others for future payment, such as a bond or a bank deposit is an asset.
Goodwill	Goodwill is an important accounting concept that describes the value of a business entity not directly attributable to its tangible assets and liabilities.
Intangible asset	An intangible assets is defined as an asset that is not physical in nature. The most common types are trade secrets (e.g., customer lists and know-how), copyrights, patents, trademarks, and goodwill.
Receiver	A person that is appointed as a custodian of other people's property by a court of law or a creditor of the owner, pending a lawsuit or reorganization is called a receiver.
Body language	Body language is a broad term for forms of communication using body movements or gestures instead of, or in addition to, sounds, verbal language, or other forms of communication.
Privilege	Generally, a legal right to engage in conduct that would otherwise result in legal liability is a privilege. Privileges are commonly classified as absolute or conditional. Occasionally, privilege is also used to denote a legal right to refrain from particular behavior.
Preference	The act of a debtor in paying or securing one or more of his creditors in a manner more favorable to them than to other creditors or to the exclusion of such other creditors is a preference. In the absence of statute, a preference is perfectly good, but to be legal it must be bona fide, and not a mere subterfuge of the debtor to secure a future benefit to himself or to prevent the application of his property to his debts.
Personal saving	Personal saving refers to the personal income of households less personal taxes and personal consumption expenditures; disposable income not spent for consumer goods.
Credibility	The extent to which a source is perceived as having knowledge, skill, or experience relevant to a communication topic and can be trusted to give an unbiased opinion or present objective information on the issue is called credibility.
Service	Service refers to a "non tangible product" that is not embodied in a physical good and that typically effects some change in another product, person, or institution. Contrasts with good.

Advertisement	Advertisement is the promotion of goods, services, companies and ideas, usually by an identified sponsor. Marketers see advertising as part of an overall promotional strategy.
Complaint	The pleading in a civil case in which the plaintiff states his claim and requests relief is called complaint. In the common law, it is a formal legal document that sets out the basic facts and legal reasons that the filing party (the plaintiffs) believes are sufficient to support a claim against another person, persons, entity or entities (the defendants) that entitles the plaintiff(s) to a remedy (either money damages or injunctive relief).
Contract	A contract is a "promise" or an "agreement" that is enforced or recognized by the law. In the civil law, a contract is considered to be part of the general law of obligations.
Welfare	Welfare refers to the economic well being of an individual, group, or economy. For individuals, it is conceptualized by a utility function. For groups, including countries and the world, it is a tricky philosophical concept, since individuals fare differently.
Dividend	Amount of corporate profits paid out for each share of stock is referred to as dividend.
Policy	Similar to a script in that a policy can be a less than completely rational decision-making method. Involves the use of a pre-existing set of decision steps for any problem that presents itself.
Customer value	Customer value refers to the unique combination of benefits received by targeted buyers that includes quality, price, convenience, on-time delivery, and both before-sale and after-sale service.
Attachment	Attachment in general, the process of taking a person's property under an appropriate judicial order by an appropriate officer of the court. Used for a variety of purposes, including the acquisition of jurisdiction over the property seized and the securing of property that may be used to satisfy a debt.
Brand	A name, symbol, or design that identifies the goods or services of one seller or group of sellers and distinguishes them from the goods and services of competitors is a brand.
Firm	An organization that employs resources to produce a good or service for profit and owns and operates one or more plants is referred to as a firm.
Discount	The difference between the face value of a bond and its selling price, when a bond is sold for less than its face value it's referred to as a discount.
Invoice	The itemized bill for a transaction, stating the nature of the transaction and its cost. In international trade, the invoice price is often the preferred basis for levying an ad valorem tariff.
Tangible	Having a physical existence is referred to as the tangible. Personal property other than real estate, such as cars, boats, stocks, or other assets.
Promotion	Promotion refers to all the techniques sellers use to motivate people to buy products or services. An attempt by marketers to inform people about products and to persuade them to participate in an exchange.
Credit	Credit refers to a recording as positive in the balance of payments, any transaction that gives rise to a payment into the country, such as an export, the sale of an asset, or borrowing from abroad.
Franchise	A contractual right to sell certain products or services, use certain trademarks, or perform activities in a geographical region is called a franchise.
Purchasing	Purchasing refers to the function in a firm that searches for quality material resources, finds the best suppliers, and negotiates the best price for goods and services.

Committee	A long-lasting, sometimes permanent team in the organization structure created to deal with tasks that recur regularly is the committee.
Capital	Capital generally refers to financial wealth, especially that used to start or maintain a business. In classical economics, capital is one of four factors of production, the others being land and labor and entrepreneurship.
Appreciation	Appreciation refers to a rise in the value of a country's currency on the exchange market, relative either to a particular other currency or to a weighted average of other currencies. The currency is said to appreciate. Opposite of 'depreciation.' Appreciation can also refer to the increase in value of any asset.
Fund	Independent accounting entity with a self-balancing set of accounts segregated for the purposes of carrying on specific activities is referred to as a fund.
Leadership	Management merely consists of leadership applied to business situations; or in other words: management forms a sub-set of the broader process of leadership.
Supply	Supply is the aggregate amount of any material good that can be called into being at a certain price point; it comprises one half of the equation of supply and demand. In classical economic theory, a curve representing supply is one of the factors that produce price.
Sales promotion	Sales promotion refers to the promotional tool that stimulates consumer purchasing and dealer interest by means of short-term activities.
Stock	In financial terminology, stock is the capital raized by a corporation, through the issuance and sale of shares.
Personnel	A collective term for all of the employees of an organization. Personnel is also commonly used to refer to the personnel management function or the organizational unit responsible for administering personnel programs.
Credit union	A credit union is a not-for-profit co-operative financial institution that is owned and controlled by its members, through the election of a volunteer Board of Directors elected from the membership itself.
Union	A worker association that bargains with employers over wages and working conditions is called a union.
Points	Loan origination fees that may be deductible as interest by a buyer of property. A seller of property who pays points reduces the selling price by the amount of the points paid for the buyer.
Incentive	An incentive is any factor (financial or non-financial) that provides a motive for a particular course of action, or counts as a reason for preferring one choice to the alternatives.
Recovery	Characterized by rizing output, falling unemployment, rizing profits, and increasing economic activity following a decline is a recovery.
Coupon	In finance, a coupon is "attached" to a bond, either physically (as with old bonds) or electronically. Each coupon represents a predetermined payment promized to the bond-holder in return for his or her loan of money to the bond-issuer. .
Effective communication	When the intended meaning equals the perceived meaning it is called effective communication.
Quality management	Quality management is a method for ensuring that all the activities necessary to design, develop and implement a product or service are effective and efficient with respect to the system and its performance.

Go to **Cram101.com** for the Practice Tests for this Chapter.

Warranty	An obligation of a company to replace defective goods or correct any deficiencies in performance or quality of a product is called a warranty.
Customer service	The ability of logistics management to satisfy users in terms of time, dependability, communication, and convenience is called the customer service.
Portfolio	In finance, a portfolio is a collection of investments held by an institution or a private individual. Holding but not always a portfolio is part of an investment and risk-limiting strategy called diversification. By owning several assets, certain types of risk (in particular specific risk) can be reduced.
Draft	A signed, written order by which one party instructs another party to pay a specified sum to a third party, at sight or at a specific date is a draft.
Assignment	A transfer of property or some right or interest is referred to as assignment.
Graduation	Termination of a country's eligibility for GSP tariff preferences on the grounds that it has progressed sufficiently, in terms of per capita income or another measure, that it is no longer in need to special and differential treatment is graduation.
National bank	A National bank refers to federally chartered banks. They are an ordinary private bank which operates nationally (as opposed to regionally or locally or even internationally).
General manager	A manager who is responsible for several departments that perform different functions is called general manager.
Auction	A preexisting business model that operates successfully on the Internet by announcing an item for sale and permitting multiple purchasers to bid on them under specified rules and condition is an auction.
Corporation	A legal entity chartered by a state or the Federal government that is distinct and separate from the individuals who own it is a corporation. This separation gives the corporation unique powers which other legal entities lack.
Production	The creation of finished goods and services using the factors of production: land, labor, capital, entrepreneurship, and knowledge.
Industry	A group of firms that produce identical or similar products is an industry. It is also used specifically to refer to an area of economic production focused on manufacturing which involves large amounts of capital investment before any profit can be realized, also called "heavy industry".
Economic development	Increase in the economic standard of living of a country's population, normally accomplished by increasing its stocks of physical and human capital and improving its technology is an economic development.
Production line	A production line is a set of sequential operations established in a factory whereby materials are put through a refining process to produce an end-product that is suitable for onward consumption; or components are assembled to make a finished article.
Operation	A standardized method or technique that is performed repetitively, often on different materials resulting in different finished goods is called an operation.
Marketing	Promoting and selling products or services to customers, or prospective customers, is referred to as marketing.
Foundation	A Foundation is a type of philanthropic organization set up by either individuals or institutions as a legal entity (either as a corporation or trust) with the purpose of distributing grants to support causes in line with the goals of the foundation.
Dealer	People who link buyers with sellers by buying and selling securities at stated prices are

Go to **Cram101.com** for the Practice Tests for this Chapter.

referred to as a dealer.

Go to **Cram101.com** for the Practice Tests for this Chapter.
And, **NEVER** highlight a book again!

Appreciation	Appreciation refers to a rise in the value of a country's currency on the exchange market, relative either to a particular other currency or to a weighted average of other currencies. The currency is said to appreciate. Opposite of 'depreciation.' Appreciation can also refer to the increase in value of any asset.
Advertising	Advertising refers to paid, nonpersonal communication through various media by organizations and individuals who are in some way identified in the advertising message.
Advertising manager	The individual in an organization who is responsible for the planning, coordinating, budgeting, and implementing of the advertising program is an advertising manager.
Firm	An organization that employs resources to produce a good or service for profit and owns and operates one or more plants is referred to as a firm.
General manager	A manager who is responsible for several departments that perform different functions is called general manager.
Service	Service refers to a "non tangible product" that is not embodied in a physical good and that typically effects some change in another product, person, or institution. Contrasts with good.
Loyalty	Marketers tend to define customer loyalty as making repeat purchases. Some argue that it should be defined attitudinally as a strongly positive feeling about the brand.
Customer service	The ability of logistics management to satisfy users in terms of time, dependability, communication, and convenience is called the customer service.
Complaint	The pleading in a civil case in which the plaintiff states his claim and requests relief is called complaint. In the common law, it is a formal legal document that sets out the basic facts and legal reasons that the filing party (the plaintiffs) believes are sufficient to support a claim against another person, persons, entity or entities (the defendants) that entitles the plaintiff(s) to a remedy (either money damages or injunctive relief).
Goodwill	Goodwill is an important accounting concept that describes the value of a business entity not directly attributable to its tangible assets and liabilities.
Credit	Credit refers to a recording as positive in the balance of payments, any transaction that gives rise to a payment into the country, such as an export, the sale of an asset, or borrowing from abroad.
Policy	Similar to a script in that a policy can be a less than completely rational decision-making method. Involves the use of a pre-existing set of decision steps for any problem that presents itself.
Quick response	An inventory management system designed to reduce the retailer's lead-time, thereby lowering its inventory investment, improving customer service levels, and reducing logistics expense is referred to as quick response.
Supervisor	A Supervisor is an employee of an organization with some of the powers and responsibilities of management, occupying a role between true manager and a regular employee. A Supervisor position is typically the first step towards being promoted into a management role.
Verification	Verification refers to the final stage of the creative process where the validity or truthfulness of the insight is determined. The feedback portion of communication in which the receiver sends a message to the source indicating receipt of the message and the degree to which he or she understood the message.
Writ	Writ refers to a commandment of a court given for the purpose of compelling certain action from the defendant, and usually executed by a sheriff or other judicial officer.
Trust	An arrangement in which shareholders of independent firms agree to give up their stock in

exchange for trust certificates that entitle them to a share of the trust's common profits.

Confirmed	When the seller's bank agrees to assume liability on the letter of credit issued by the buyer's bank the transaction is confirmed. The term means that the credit is not only backed up by the issuing foreign bank, but that payment is also guaranteed by the notifying American bank.
Journal	Book of original entry, in which transactions are recorded in a general ledger system, is referred to as a journal.
Receiver	A person that is appointed as a custodian of other people's property by a court of law or a creditor of the owner, pending a lawsuit or reorganization is called a receiver.
Personnel	A collective term for all of the employees of an organization. Personnel is also commonly used to refer to the personnel management function or the organizational unit responsible for administering personnel programs.
Commerce	Commerce is the exchange of something of value between two entities. It is the central mechanism from which capitalism is derived.
Exchange	The trade of things of value between buyer and seller so that each is better off after the trade is called the exchange.
Property	Assets defined in the broadest legal sense. Property includes the unrealized receivables of a cash basis taxpayer, but not services rendered.
Brief	Brief refers to a statement of a party's case or legal arguments, usually prepared by an attorney. Also used to make legal arguments before appellate courts.
Specialist	A specialist is a trader who makes a market in one or several stocks and holds the limit order book for those stocks.
Contract	A contract is a "promise" or an "agreement" that is enforced or recognized by the law. In the civil law, a contract is considered to be part of the general law of obligations.
Expense	In accounting, an expense represents an event in which an asset is used up or a liability is incurred. In terms of the accounting equation, expenses reduce owners' equity.
Technology	The body of knowledge and techniques that can be used to combine economic resources to produce goods and services is called technology.
Contribution	In business organization law, the cash or property contributed to a business by its owners is referred to as contribution.
Accommodation	Accommodation is a term used to describe a delivery of nonconforming goods meant as a partial performance of a contract for the sale of goods, where a full performance is not possible.
Accord	An agreement whereby the parties agree to accept something different in satisfaction of the original contract is an accord.
Purchasing	Purchasing refers to the function in a firm that searches for quality material resources, finds the best suppliers, and negotiates the best price for goods and services.
Closing	The finalization of a real estate sales transaction that passes title to the property from the seller to the buyer is referred to as a closing. Closing is a sales term which refers to the process of making a sale. It refers to reaching the final step, which may be an exchange of money or acquiring a signature.
Interest	In finance and economics, interest is the price paid by a borrower for the use of a lender's money. In other words, interest is the amount of paid to "rent" money for a period of time.
Points	Loan origination fees that may be deductible as interest by a buyer of property. A seller of

Go to **Cram101.com** for the Practice Tests for this Chapter.

property who pays points reduces the selling price by the amount of the points paid for the buyer.

Broker	In commerce, a broker is a party that mediates between a buyer and a seller. A broker who also acts as a seller or as a buyer becomes a principal party to the deal.
Dealer	People who link buyers with sellers by buying and selling securities at stated prices are referred to as a dealer.
American Airlines	American Airlines developed from a conglomeration of about 82 small airlines through a series of corporate acquisitions and reorganizations: initially, the name American Airways was used as a common brand by a number of independent air carriers. American Airlines is the largest airline in the world in terms of total passengers transported and fleet size, and the second-largest airline in the world.
Market timing	Market timing is the strategy of making buy or sell decisions of financial assets (often stocks) by attempting to predict future market price movements. The prediction may be based on an outlook of market or economic conditions resulting from technical or fundamental analysis. This is an investment strategy based on the outlook for an aggregate market, rather than for a particular financial asset.
Market	A market is, as defined in economics, a social arrangement that allows buyers and sellers to discover information and carry out a voluntary exchange of goods or services.
Marketing	Promoting and selling products or services to customers, or prospective customers, is referred to as marketing.
Public relations	Public relations refers to the management function that evaluates public attitudes, changes policies and procedures in response to the public's requests, and executes a program of action and information to earn public understanding and acceptance.
Layout	Layout refers to the physical arrangement of the various parts of an advertisement including the headline, subheads, illustrations, body copy, and any identifying marks.
Industry	A group of firms that produce identical or similar products is an industry. It is also used specifically to refer to an area of economic production focused on manufacturing which involves large amounts of capital investment before any profit can be realized, also called "heavy industry".
Promotion	Promotion refers to all the techniques sellers use to motivate people to buy products or services. An attempt by marketers to inform people about products and to persuade them to participate in an exchange.
Preparation	Preparation refers to usually the first stage in the creative process. It includes education and formal training.
Small business	Small business refers to a business that is independently owned and operated, is not dominant in its field of operation, and meets certain standards of size in terms of employees or annual receipts.
Aid	Assistance provided by countries and by international institutions such as the World Bank to developing countries in the form of monetary grants, loans at low interest rates, in kind, or a combination of these is called aid. Aid can also refer to assistance of any type rendered to benefit some group or individual.
International Business	International business refers to any firm that engages in international trade or investment.
American Express	From the early 1980s until the late 1990s, American Express was known for cutting its merchant fees (also known as a "discount rate") to fine merchants and restaurants if they

Go to **Cram101.com** for the Practice Tests for this Chapter.

only accepted American Express and no other credit or charge cards. This prompted competitors such as Visa and MasterCard to cry foul for a while, as the tactics "locked" restaurants into American Express.

Supply

Supply is the aggregate amount of any material good that can be called into being at a certain price point; it comprises one half of the equation of supply and demand. In classical economic theory, a curve representing supply is one of the factors that produce price.

Draft

A signed, written order by which one party instructs another party to pay a specified sum to a third party, at sight or at a specific date is a draft.

Warranty

An obligation of a company to replace defective goods or correct any deficiencies in performance or quality of a product is called a warranty.

Credit	Credit refers to a recording as positive in the balance of payments, any transaction that gives rise to a payment into the country, such as an export, the sale of an asset, or borrowing from abroad.
Option	A contract that gives the purchaser the option to buy or sell the underlying financial instrument at a specified price, called the exercise price or strike price, within a specific period of time.
Advertising	Advertising refers to paid, nonpersonal communication through various media by organizations and individuals who are in some way identified in the advertising message.
Firm	An organization that employs resources to produce a good or service for profit and owns and operates one or more plants is referred to as a firm.
Supervisor	A Supervisor is an employee of an organization with some of the powers and responsibilities of management, occupying a role between true manager and a regular employee. A Supervisor position is typically the first step towards being promoted into a management role.
Operation	A standardized method or technique that is performed repetitively, often on different materials resulting in different finished goods is called an operation.
Service	Service refers to a "non tangible product" that is not embodied in a physical good and that typically effects some change in another product, person, or institution. Contrasts with good.
Mistake	In contract law a mistake is incorrect understanding by one or more parties to a contract and may be used as grounds to invalidate the agreement. Common law has identified three different types of mistake in contract: unilateral mistake, mutual mistake, and common mistake.
Complaint	The pleading in a civil case in which the plaintiff states his claim and requests relief is called complaint. In the common law, it is a formal legal document that sets out the basic facts and legal reasons that the filing party (the plaintiffs) believes are sufficient to support a claim against another person, persons, entity or entities (the defendants) that entitles the plaintiff(s) to a remedy (either money damages or injunctive relief).
Exchange	The trade of things of value between buyer and seller so that each is better off after the trade is called the exchange.
Policy	Similar to a script in that a policy can be a less than completely rational decision-making method. Involves the use of a pre-existing set of decision steps for any problem that presents itself.
Warranty	An obligation of a company to replace defective goods or correct any deficiencies in performance or quality of a product is called a warranty.
Customer service	The ability of logistics management to satisfy users in terms of time, dependability, communication, and convenience is called the customer service.
Grant	Grant refers to an intergovernmental transfer of funds . Since the New Deal, state and local governments have become increasingly dependent upon federal grants for an almost infinite variety of programs.
Goodwill	Goodwill is an important accounting concept that describes the value of a business entity not directly attributable to its tangible assets and liabilities.
Invoice	The itemized bill for a transaction, stating the nature of the transaction and its cost. In international trade, the invoice price is often the preferred basis for levying an ad valorem tariff.
Credibility	The extent to which a source is perceived as having knowledge, skill, or experience relevant to a communication topic and can be trusted to give an unbiased opinion or present objective

	information on the issue is called credibility.
Receiver	A person that is appointed as a custodian of other people's property by a court of law or a creditor of the owner, pending a lawsuit or reorganization is called a receiver.
Adjuster	A person who settles insurance claims by calculating the amount of loss or damage is an adjuster. This person may work for the insurance company or an independent adjusting company.
Interest	In finance and economics, interest is the price paid by a borrower for the use of a lender's money. In other words, interest is the amount of paid to "rent" money for a period of time.
Asset	An item of property, such as land, capital, money, a share in ownership, or a claim on others for future payment, such as a bond or a bank deposit is an asset.
Customer satisfaction	Customer satisfaction is a business term which is used to capture the idea of measuring how satisfied an enterprise's customers are with the organization's efforts in a marketplace.
Personnel	A collective term for all of the employees of an organization. Personnel is also commonly used to refer to the personnel management function or the organizational unit responsible for administering personnel programs.
Appeal	Appeal refers to the act of asking an appellate court to overturn a decision after the trial court's final judgment has been entered.
Closing	The finalization of a real estate sales transaction that passes title to the property from the seller to the buyer is referred to as a closing. Closing is a sales term which refers to the process of making a sale. It refers to reaching the final step, which may be an exchange of money or acquiring a signature.
Verification	Verification refers to the final stage of the creative process where the validity or truthfulness of the insight is determined. The feedback portion of communication in which the receiver sends a message to the source indicating receipt of the message and the degree to which he or she understood the message.
Production	The creation of finished goods and services using the factors of production: land, labor, capital, entrepreneurship, and knowledge.
Consideration	Consideration in contract law, a basic requirement for an enforceable agreement under traditional contract principles, defined in this text as legal value, bargained for and given in exchange for an act or promise. In corporation law, cash or property contributed to a corporation in exchange for shares, or a promise to contribute such cash or property.
Writ	Writ refers to a commandment of a court given for the purpose of compelling certain action from the defendant, and usually executed by a sheriff or other judicial officer.
Compromise	Compromise occurs when the interaction is moderately important to meeting goals and the goals are neither completely compatible nor completely incompatible.
Labor	People's physical and mental talents and efforts that are used to help produce goods and services are called labor.
Cooperative	A business owned and controlled by the people who use it, producers, consumers, or workers with similar needs who pool their resources for mutual gain is called cooperative.
Pledge	In law a pledge (also pawn) is a bailment of personal property as a security for some debt or engagement.
Graduation	Termination of a country's eligibility for GSP tariff preferences on the grounds that it has progressed sufficiently, in terms of per capita income or another measure, that it is no longer in need to special and differential treatment is graduation.
Supply	Supply is the aggregate amount of any material good that can be called into being at a

certain price point; it comprises one half of the equation of supply and demand. In classical economic theory, a curve representing supply is one of the factors that produce price.

Stock	In financial terminology, stock is the capital raized by a corporation, through the issuance and sale of shares.
Trial	An examination before a competent tribunal, according to the law of the land, of the facts or law put in issue in a cause, for the purpose of determining such issue is a trial. When the court hears and determines any issue of fact or law for the purpose of determining the rights of the parties, it may be considered a trial.
Security	Security refers to a claim on the borrower future income that is sold by the borrower to the lender. A security is a type of transferable interest representing financial value.
Sales tax	A sales tax is a tax on consumption. It is normally a certain percentage that is added onto the price of a good or service that is purchased.
Corporation	A legal entity chartered by a state or the Federal government that is distinct and separate from the individuals who own it is a corporation. This separation gives the corporation unique powers which other legal entities lack.
Cabinet	The heads of the executive departments of a jurisdiction who report to and advise its chief executive; examples would include the president's cabinet, the governor's cabinet, and the mayor's cabinet.
Warrant	A warrant is a security that entitles the holder to buy or sell a certain additional quantity of an underlying security at an agreed-upon price, at the holder's discretion.
Contract	A contract is a "promise" or an "agreement" that is enforced or recognized by the law. In the civil law, a contract is considered to be part of the general law of obligations.

Exchange	The trade of things of value between buyer and seller so that each is better off after the trade is called the exchange.
Industry	A group of firms that produce identical or similar products is an industry. It is also used specifically to refer to an area of economic production focused on manufacturing which involves large amounts of capital investment before any profit can be realized, also called "heavy industry".
Fob shipping point	Fob shipping point refers to freight terms indicating that the goods are placed free on board the carrier by the seller, and the buyer pays the freight cost; goods belong to the buyer while in transit.
Invoice	The itemized bill for a transaction, stating the nature of the transaction and its cost. In international trade, the invoice price is often the preferred basis for levying an ad valorem tariff.
Policy	Similar to a script in that a policy can be a less than completely rational decision-making method. Involves the use of a pre-existing set of decision steps for any problem that presents itself.
Mistake	In contract law a mistake is incorrect understanding by one or more parties to a contract and may be used as grounds to invalidate the agreement. Common law has identified three different types of mistake in contract: unilateral mistake, mutual mistake, and common mistake.
Brainstorming	Brainstorming refers to a technique designed to overcome our natural tendency to evaluate and criticize ideas and thereby reduce the creative output of those ideas. People are encouraged to produce ideas/options without criticizing, often at a very fast pace to minimize our natural tendency to criticize.
Goodwill	Goodwill is an important accounting concept that describes the value of a business entity not directly attributable to its tangible assets and liabilities.
Interest	In finance and economics, interest is the price paid by a borrower for the use of a lender's money. In other words, interest is the amount of paid to "rent" money for a period of time.
Personnel	A collective term for all of the employees of an organization. Personnel is also commonly used to refer to the personnel management function or the organizational unit responsible for administering personnel programs.
Security	Security refers to a claim on the borrower future income that is sold by the borrower to the lender. A security is a type of transferable interest representing financial value.
Social Security	Social security primarily refers to a field of social welfare concerned with social protection, or protection against socially recognized conditions, including poverty, old age, disability, unemployment, families with children and others.
Property	Assets defined in the broadest legal sense. Property includes the unrealized receivables of a cash basis taxpayer, but not services rendered.
Complete information	Complete information refers to the assumption that economic agents know everything that they need to know in order to make optimal decisions. Types of incomplete information are uncertainty and asymmetric information.
Brief	Brief refers to a statement of a party's case or legal arguments, usually prepared by an attorney. Also used to make legal arguments before appellate courts.
Points	Loan origination fees that may be deductible as interest by a buyer of property. A seller of property who pays points reduces the selling price by the amount of the points paid for the buyer.
Petition	A petition is a request to an authority, most commonly a government official or public

entity. In the colloquial sense, a petition is a document addressed to some official and signed by numerous individuals.

Consideration	Consideration in contract law, a basic requirement for an enforceable agreement under traditional contract principles, defined in this text as legal value, bargained for and given in exchange for an act or promise. In corporation law, cash or property contributed to a corporation in exchange for shares, or a promise to contribute such cash or property.
Credibility	The extent to which a source is perceived as having knowledge, skill, or experience relevant to a communication topic and can be trusted to give an unbiased opinion or present objective information on the issue is called credibility.
Committee	A long-lasting, sometimes permanent team in the organization structure created to deal with tasks that recur regularly is the committee.
Hearing	A hearing is a proceeding before a court or other decision-making body or officer. A hearing is generally distinguished from a trial in that it is usually shorter and often less formal.
Service	Service refers to a "non tangible product" that is not embodied in a physical good and that typically effects some change in another product, person, or institution. Contrasts with good.
Appreciation	Appreciation refers to a rise in the value of a country's currency on the exchange market, relative either to a particular other currency or to a weighted average of other currencies. The currency is said to appreciate. Opposite of 'depreciation.' Appreciation can also refer to the increase in value of any asset.
Red tape	Red tape is a derisive term for excessive regulations or rigid conformity to formal rules that are considered redundant or bureaucratic and hinders or prevents action or decision-making.
Rebuttal	Testimony addressed to evidence produced by the opposite party is referred to as rebuttal.
Expense	In accounting, an expense represents an event in which an asset is used up or a liability is incurred. In terms of the accounting equation, expenses reduce owners' equity.
Argument	The discussion by counsel for the respective parties of their contentions on the law and the facts of the case being tried in order to aid the jury in arriving at a correct and just conclusion is called argument.
Aid	Assistance provided by countries and by international institutions such as the World Bank to developing countries in the form of monetary grants, loans at low interest rates, in kind, or a combination of these is called aid. Aid can also refer to assistance of any type rendered to benefit some group or individual.
Welfare	Welfare refers to the economic well being of an individual, group, or economy. For individuals, it is conceptualized by a utility function. For groups, including countries and the world, it is a tricky philosophical concept, since individuals fare differently.
Administrator	Administrator refers to the personal representative appointed by a probate court to settle the estate of a deceased person who died.
Appeal	Appeal refers to the act of asking an appellate court to overturn a decision after the trial court's final judgment has been entered.
Leadership	Management merely consists of leadership applied to business situations; or in other words: management forms a sub-set of the broader process of leadership.
Budget	Budget refers to an account, usually for a year, of the planned expenditures and the expected receipts of an entity. For a government, the receipts are tax revenues.

Merchandising	Merchandising refers to the business of acquiring finished goods for resale, either in a wholesale or a retail operation.
Buyer	A buyer refers to a role in the buying center with formal authority and responsibility to select the supplier and negotiate the terms of the contract.
Budget committee	A group of top-management personnel who advise the budget director during the preparation of the budget is a budget committee.
Compliance	A type of influence process where a receiver accepts the position advocated by a source to obtain favorable outcomes or to avoid punishment is the compliance.
Closing	The finalization of a real estate sales transaction that passes title to the property from the seller to the buyer is referred to as a closing. Closing is a sales term which refers to the process of making a sale. It refers to reaching the final step, which may be an exchange of money or acquiring a signature.
Targeting	In advertizing, targeting is to select a demographic or other group of people to advertise to, and create advertisements appropriately.
Target audience	That group that composes the present and potential prospects for a product or service is called the target audience.
Direct sale	A direct sale is a sale to customers through distributors or self-employed sales people rather than through shops. Includes both personal contact with consumers in their homes (and other nonstore locations such as offices) and phone solicitations initiated by a retailer.
Promotion	Promotion refers to all the techniques sellers use to motivate people to buy products or services. An attempt by marketers to inform people about products and to persuade them to participate in an exchange.
Coupon	In finance, a coupon is "attached" to a bond, either physically (as with old bonds) or electronically. Each coupon represents a predetermined payment promized to the bond-holder in return for his or her loan of money to the bond-issuer. .
Real value	Real value is the value of anything expressed in money of the day with the effects of inflation removed.
Drawback	Drawback refers to rebate of import duties when the imported good is re-exported or used as input to the production of an exported good.
Insurance	Insurance refers to a system by which individuals can reduce their exposure to risk of large losses by spreading the risks among a large number of persons.
Purchasing	Purchasing refers to the function in a firm that searches for quality material resources, finds the best suppliers, and negotiates the best price for goods and services.
Capital	Capital generally refers to financial wealth, especially that used to start or maintain a business. In classical economics, capital is one of four factors of production, the others being land and labor and entrepreneurship.
Certificates of deposit	Certificates of deposit refer to a certificate offered by banks, savings and loans, and other financial institutions for the deposit of funds at a given interest rate over a specified time period.
Principal	In agency law, one under whose direction an agent acts and for whose benefit that agent acts is a principal.
Balance	In banking and accountancy, the outstanding balance is the amount of money owned, (or due), that remains in a deposit account (or a loan account) at a given date, after all past remittances, payments and withdrawal have been accounted for. It can be positive (then, in

Go to **Cram101.com** for the Practice Tests for this Chapter.

the balance sheet of a firm, it is an asset) or negative (a liability).

Annuity	A contract to make regular payments to a person for life or for a fixed period is an annuity.
Gain	In finance, gain is a profit or an increase in value of an investment such as a stock or bond. Gain is calculated by fair market value or the proceeds from the sale of the investment minus the sum of the purchase price and all costs associated with it.
Contract	A contract is a "promise" or an "agreement" that is enforced or recognized by the law. In the civil law, a contract is considered to be part of the general law of obligations.
Death benefit	A payment made by an employer to the beneficiary or beneficiaries of a deceased employee as a result of the death of the employee is a death benefit.
Beneficiary	The person for whose benefit an insurance policy, trust, will, or contract is established is a beneficiary. In the case of a contract, the beneficiary is called a third-party beneficiary.
Mutual fund	A mutual fund is a form of collective investment that pools money from many investors and invests the money in stocks, bonds, short-term money market instruments, and/or other securities. In a mutual fund, the fund manager trades the fund's underlying securities, realizing capital gains or loss, and collects the dividend or interest income.
Option	A contract that gives the purchaser the option to buy or sell the underlying financial instrument at a specified price, called the exercise price or strike price, within a specific period of time.
Stock	In financial terminology, stock is the capital raized by a corporation, through the issuance and sale of shares.
Bond	Bond refers to a debt instrument, issued by a borrower and promising a specified stream of payments to the purchaser, usually regular interest payments plus a final repayment of principal.
Fund	Independent accounting entity with a self-balancing set of accounts segregated for the purposes of carrying on specific activities is referred to as a fund.
Objection	In the trial of a case the formal remonstrance made by counsel to something that has been said or done, in order to obtain the court's ruling thereon is an objection.
Tangible	Having a physical existence is referred to as the tangible. Personal property other than real estate, such as cars, boats, stocks, or other assets.
Trial	An examination before a competent tribunal, according to the law of the land, of the facts or law put in issue in a cause, for the purpose of determining such issue is a trial. When the court hears and determines any issue of fact or law for the purpose of determining the rights of the parties, it may be considered a trial.
Testimonial	Testimonial refers to a statement by a public figure professing the merits of some product or service.
Incentive	An incentive is any factor (financial or non-financial) that provides a motive for a particular course of action, or counts as a reason for preferring one choice to the alternatives.
Dealer	People who link buyers with sellers by buying and selling securities at stated prices are referred to as a dealer.
Agent	A person who makes economic decisions for another economic actor. A hired manager operates as an agent for a firm's owner.
Profit	Profit refers to the return to the resource entrepreneurial ability; total revenue minus

total cost.

Turnover	Turnover in a financial context refers to the rate at which a provider of goods cycles through its average inventory. Turnover in a human resources context refers to the characteristic of a given company or industry, relative to rate at which an employer gains and loses staff.
Markup	Markup is a term used in marketing to indicate how much the price of a product is above the cost of producing and distributing the product.
Marketing	Promoting and selling products or services to customers, or prospective customers, is referred to as marketing.
Publicity	Publicity refers to any information about an individual, product, or organization that's distributed to the public through the media and that's not paid for or controlled by the seller.
Writ	Writ refers to a commandment of a court given for the purpose of compelling certain action from the defendant, and usually executed by a sheriff or other judicial officer.
Sales promotion	Sales promotion refers to the promotional tool that stimulates consumer purchasing and dealer interest by means of short-term activities.
Advertising	Advertising refers to paid, nonpersonal communication through various media by organizations and individuals who are in some way identified in the advertising message.
Market	A market is, as defined in economics, a social arrangement that allows buyers and sellers to discover information and carry out a voluntary exchange of goods or services.
Capital gain	Capital gain refers to the gain in value that the owner of an asset experiences when the price of the asset rises, including when the currency in which the asset is denominated appreciates.
Exempt	Employees who are not covered by the Fair Labor Standards Act are exempt. Exempt employees are not eligible for overtime pay.
Warranty	An obligation of a company to replace defective goods or correct any deficiencies in performance or quality of a product is called a warranty.
General manager	A manager who is responsible for several departments that perform different functions is called general manager.

Supply	Supply is the aggregate amount of any material good that can be called into being at a certain price point; it comprises one half of the equation of supply and demand. In classical economic theory, a curve representing supply is one of the factors that produce price.
Interest	In finance and economics, interest is the price paid by a borrower for the use of a lender's money. In other words, interest is the amount of paid to "rent" money for a period of time.
Boot	Boot is any type of personal property received in a real property transaction that is not like kind, such as cash, mortgage notes, a boat or stock. The exchanger pays taxes on the boot to the extent of recognized capital gain. In an exchange if any funds are not used in purchasing the replacement property, that also will be called boot.
Dealer	People who link buyers with sellers by buying and selling securities at stated prices are referred to as a dealer.
Stock	In financial terminology, stock is the capital raized by a corporation, through the issuance and sale of shares.
Service	Service refers to a "non tangible product" that is not embodied in a physical good and that typically effects some change in another product, person, or institution. Contrasts with good.
Technology	The body of knowledge and techniques that can be used to combine economic resources to produce goods and services is called technology.
Market	A market is, as defined in economics, a social arrangement that allows buyers and sellers to discover information and carry out a voluntary exchange of goods or services.
Buyer	A buyer refers to a role in the buying center with formal authority and responsibility to select the supplier and negotiate the terms of the contract.
Postal Service	The postal service was created in Philadelphia under Benjamin Franklin on July 26, 1775 by decree of the Second Continental Congress. Based on a clause in the United States Constitution empowering Congress "To establish Post Offices and post Roads."
United States Postal Service	The United States Postal Service is an "independent establishment of the executive branch" of the United States government. It is the third-largest employer in the United States (after the United States Department of Defense and Wal-Mart) and operates the largest civilian vehicle fleet in the world, with an estimated 260,000 vehicles.
Sales tax	A sales tax is a tax on consumption. It is normally a certain percentage that is added onto the price of a good or service that is purchased.
Contract	A contract is a "promise" or an "agreement" that is enforced or recognized by the law. In the civil law, a contract is considered to be part of the general law of obligations.
Preference	The act of a debtor in paying or securing one or more of his creditors in a manner more favorable to them than to other creditors or to the exclusion of such other creditors is a preference. In the absence of statute, a preference is perfectly good, but to be legal it must be bona fide, and not a mere subterfuge of the debtor to secure a future benefit to himself or to prevent the application of his property to his debts.
Fob shipping point	Fob shipping point refers to freight terms indicating that the goods are placed free on board the carrier by the seller, and the buyer pays the freight cost; goods belong to the buyer while in transit.
Fob destination	Fob destination refers to freight terms indicating that the goods are placed free on board at the buyer's place of business, and the seller pays the freight cost; goods belong to the seller while in transit.
Credit	Credit refers to a recording as positive in the balance of payments, any transaction that

Go to **Cram101.com** for the Practice Tests for this Chapter.

	gives rise to a payment into the country, such as an export, the sale of an asset, or borrowing from abroad.
Free On Board	Free On Board is an Incoterm. It means that the seller pays for transportation of the goods to the port of shipment, plus loading costs. The buyer pays freight, insurance, unloading costs and transportation from the port of destination to his factory. The passing of risks occurs when the goods pass the ship's rail at the port of shipment.
Security	Security refers to a claim on the borrower future income that is sold by the borrower to the lender. A security is a type of transferable interest representing financial value.
Firm	An organization that employs resources to produce a good or service for profit and owns and operates one or more plants is referred to as a firm.
Invoice	The itemized bill for a transaction, stating the nature of the transaction and its cost. In international trade, the invoice price is often the preferred basis for levying an ad valorem tariff.
Goodwill	Goodwill is an important accounting concept that describes the value of a business entity not directly attributable to its tangible assets and liabilities.
Preparation	Preparation refers to usually the first stage in the creative process. It includes education and formal training.
Quick response	An inventory management system designed to reduce the retailer's lead-time, thereby lowering its inventory investment, improving customer service levels, and reducing logistics expense is referred to as quick response.
Mistake	In contract law a mistake is incorrect understanding by one or more parties to a contract and may be used as grounds to invalidate the agreement. Common law has identified three different types of mistake in contract: unilateral mistake, mutual mistake, and common mistake.
Appreciation	Appreciation refers to a rise in the value of a country's currency on the exchange market, relative either to a particular other currency or to a weighted average of other currencies. The currency is said to appreciate. Opposite of 'depreciation.' Appreciation can also refer to the increase in value of any asset.
Corporation	A legal entity chartered by a state or the Federal government that is distinct and separate from the individuals who own it is a corporation. This separation gives the corporation unique powers which other legal entities lack.
Manufacturing	Production of goods primarily by the application of labor and capital to raw materials and other intermediate inputs, in contrast to agriculture, mining, forestry, fishing, and services a manufacturing.
Purchasing	Purchasing refers to the function in a firm that searches for quality material resources, finds the best suppliers, and negotiates the best price for goods and services.
Discount	The difference between the face value of a bond and its selling price, when a bond is sold for less than its face value it's referred to as a discount.
Exchange	The trade of things of value between buyer and seller so that each is better off after the trade is called the exchange.
Promotion	Promotion refers to all the techniques sellers use to motivate people to buy products or services. An attempt by marketers to inform people about products and to persuade them to participate in an exchange.
Applicant	In many tribunal and administrative law suits, the person who initiates the claim is called the applicant.

Standing	Standing refers to the legal requirement that anyone seeking to challenge a particular action in court must demonstrate that such action substantially affects his legitimate interests before he will be entitled to bring suit.
Creditor	A person to whom a debt or legal obligation is owed, and who has the right to enforce payment of that debt or obligation is referred to as creditor.
Asset	An item of property, such as land, capital, money, a share in ownership, or a claim on others for future payment, such as a bond or a bank deposit is an asset.
Tangible asset	Assets that have physical substance that cannot easily be converted into cash are referd to as a tangible asset.
Tangible	Having a physical existence is referred to as the tangible. Personal property other than real estate, such as cars, boats, stocks, or other assets.
Capital	Capital generally refers to financial wealth, especially that used to start or maintain a business. In classical economics, capital is one of four factors of production, the others being land and labor and entrepreneurship.
Trend	Trend refers to the long-term movement of an economic variable, such as its average rate of increase or decrease over enough years to encompass several business cycles.
Privilege	Generally, a legal right to engage in conduct that would otherwise result in legal liability is a privilege. Privileges are commonly classified as absolute or conditional. Occasionally, privilege is also used to denote a legal right to refrain from particular behavior.
Plea	A plea is an answer to a declaration or complaint or any material allegation of fact therein that, if untrue, would defeat the action. In criminal procedure, a plea is the matter that the accused, on his arraignment, alleges in answer to the charge against him.
Exchange rate	Exchange rate refers to the price at which one country's currency trades for another, typically on the exchange market.
Profit	Profit refers to the return to the resource entrepreneurial ability; total revenue minus total cost.
Credit risk	The risk of loss due to a counterparty defaulting on a contract, or more generally the risk of loss due to some "credit event" is called credit risk.
Bad debt	In accounting and finance, bad debt is the portion of receivables that can no longer be collected, typically from accounts receivable or loans. Bad debt in accounting is considered an expense.
Holding	The holding is a court's determination of a matter of law based on the issue presented in the particular case. In other words: under this law, with these facts, this result.
Appeal	Appeal refers to the act of asking an appellate court to overturn a decision after the trial court's final judgment has been entered.
Industry	A group of firms that produce identical or similar products is an industry. It is also used specifically to refer to an area of economic production focused on manufacturing which involves large amounts of capital investment before any profit can be realized, also called "heavy industry".
Hearing	A hearing is a proceeding before a court or other decision-making body or officer. A hearing is generally distinguished from a trial in that it is usually shorter and often less formal.
Policy	Similar to a script in that a policy can be a less than completely rational decision-making method. Involves the use of a pre-existing set of decision steps for any problem that presents itself.

Go to **Cram101.com** for the Practice Tests for this Chapter.

Grant	Grant refers to an intergovernmental transfer of funds . Since the New Deal, state and local governments have become increasingly dependent upon federal grants for an almost infinite variety of programs.
Marketing	Promoting and selling products or services to customers, or prospective customers, is referred to as marketing.
Coupon	In finance, a coupon is "attached" to a bond, either physically (as with old bonds) or electronically. Each coupon represents a predetermined payment promized to the bond-holder in return for his or her loan of money to the bond-issuer. .
Balance	In banking and accountancy, the outstanding balance is the amount of money owned, (or due), that remains in a deposit account (or a loan account) at a given date, after all past remittances, payments and withdrawal have been accounted for. It can be positive (then, in the balance sheet of a firm, it is an asset) or negative (a liability).
Holder	A person in possession of a document of title or an instrument payable or indorsed to him, his order, or to bearer is a holder.
Brief	Brief refers to a statement of a party's case or legal arguments, usually prepared by an attorney. Also used to make legal arguments before appellate courts.
Sales promotion	Sales promotion refers to the promotional tool that stimulates consumer purchasing and dealer interest by means of short-term activities.
Closing	The finalization of a real estate sales transaction that passes title to the property from the seller to the buyer is referred to as a closing. Closing is a sales term which refers to the process of making a sale. It refers to reaching the final step, which may be an exchange of money or acquiring a signature.

Team building	A term that describes the process of identifying roles for team members and helping the team members succeed in their roles is called team building.
Contribution	In business organization law, the cash or property contributed to a business by its owners is referred to as contribution.
Holding	The holding is a court's determination of a matter of law based on the issue presented in the particular case. In other words: under this law, with these facts, this result.
Trust	An arrangement in which shareholders of independent firms agree to give up their stock in exchange for trust certificates that entitle them to a share of the trust's common profits.
Regular meeting	A meeting held by the board of directors that is held at regular intervals at the time and place established in the bylaws is called a regular meeting.
Technology	The body of knowledge and techniques that can be used to combine economic resources to produce goods and services is called technology.
Operation	A standardized method or technique that is performed repetitively, often on different materials resulting in different finished goods is called an operation.
Trend	Trend refers to the long-term movement of an economic variable, such as its average rate of increase or decrease over enough years to encompass several business cycles.
Evaluation	The consumer's appraisal of the product or brand on important attributes is called evaluation.
Receiver	A person that is appointed as a custodian of other people's property by a court of law or a creditor of the owner, pending a lawsuit or reorganization is called a receiver.
Supervisor	A Supervisor is an employee of an organization with some of the powers and responsibilities of management, occupying a role between true manager and a regular employee. A Supervisor position is typically the first step towards being promoted into a management role.
Electronic mail	Electronic mail refers to electronic written communication between individuals using computers connected to the Internet.
Closing	The finalization of a real estate sales transaction that passes title to the property from the seller to the buyer is referred to as a closing. Closing is a sales term which refers to the process of making a sale. It refers to reaching the final step, which may be an exchange of money or acquiring a signature.
Expense	In accounting, an expense represents an event in which an asset is used up or a liability is incurred. In terms of the accounting equation, expenses reduce owners' equity.
Points	Loan origination fees that may be deductible as interest by a buyer of property. A seller of property who pays points reduces the selling price by the amount of the points paid for the buyer.
Call to action	The part of a direct response communication that makes clear to the prospect exactly what action the marketer wants to be taken is referred to as call to action.
Creep	Creep is a problem in project management where the initial objectives of the project are jeopardized by a gradual increase in overall objectives as the project progresses.
Reorganization	Reorganization occurs, among other instances, when one corporation acquires another in a merger or acquisition, a single corporation divides into two or more entities, or a corporation makes a substantial change in its capital structure.
Service	Service refers to a "non tangible product" that is not embodied in a physical good and that typically effects some change in another product, person, or institution. Contrasts with good.

Go to **Cram101.com** for the Practice Tests for this Chapter.

Go to **Cram101.com** for the Practice Tests for this Chapter.
And, **NEVER** highlight a book again!

Management	Management characterizes the process of leading and directing all or part of an organization, often a business, through the deployment and manipulation of resources. Early twentieth-century management writer Mary Parker Follett defined management as "the art of getting things done through people."
Time management	Time Management refers to tools or techniques for planning and scheduling time, usually with the aim to increase the effectiveness and/or efficiency of personal and corporate time use.
Preparation	Preparation refers to usually the first stage in the creative process. It includes education and formal training.
Authority	Authority in agency law, refers to an agent's ability to affect his principal's legal relations with third parties. Also used to refer to an actor's legal power or ability to do something. In addition, sometimes used to refer to a statute, case, or other legal source that justifies a particular result.
Operating results	Operating results refers to measures that are important to monitoring and tracking the effectiveness of a company's operations.
Financial report	Financial report refers to a written statement-also called an accountant's certificate, accountant's opinion, or audit report-prepared by an independent accountant or auditor after an audit.
Contract	A contract is a "promise" or an "agreement" that is enforced or recognized by the law. In the civil law, a contract is considered to be part of the general law of obligations.
Credit report	Information about a person's credit history that can be secured from a credit bureau is referred to as credit report.
Credit	Credit refers to a recording as positive in the balance of payments, any transaction that gives rise to a payment into the country, such as an export, the sale of an asset, or borrowing from abroad.
Audit	An examination of the financial reports to ensure that they represent what they claim and conform with generally accepted accounting principles is referred to as audit.
Accumulation	The acquisition of an increasing quantity of something. The accumulation of factors, especially capital, is a primary mechanism for economic growth.
Aid	Assistance provided by countries and by international institutions such as the World Bank to developing countries in the form of monetary grants, loans at low interest rates, in kind, or a combination of these is called aid. Aid can also refer to assistance of any type rendered to benefit some group or individual.
Firm	An organization that employs resources to produce a good or service for profit and owns and operates one or more plants is referred to as a firm.
Tenant	The party to whom the leasehold is transferred is a tenant. A leasehold estate is an ownership interest in land in which a lessee or a tenant holds real property by some form of title from a lessor or landlord.
Property	Assets defined in the broadest legal sense. Property includes the unrealized receivables of a cash basis taxpayer, but not services rendered.
Option	A contract that gives the purchaser the option to buy or sell the underlying financial instrument at a specified price, called the exercise price or strike price, within a specific period of time.
Lease	A contract for the possession and use of land or other property, including goods, on one side, and a recompense of rent or other income on the other is the lease.

Corporation	A legal entity chartered by a state or the Federal government that is distinct and separate from the individuals who own it is a corporation. This separation gives the corporation unique powers which other legal entities lack.
Enterprise	Enterprise refers to another name for a business organization. Other similar terms are business firm, sometimes simply business, sometimes simply firm, as well as company, and entity.
Lien	In its most extensive meaning, it is a charge on property for the payment or discharge of a debt or duty is referred to as lien.
Executive summary	A nontechnical summary statement designed to provide a quick overview of the full-length report on which it is based is a executive summary.
Effective communication	When the intended meaning equals the perceived meaning it is called effective communication.
Administration	Administration refers to the management and direction of the affairs of governments and institutions; a collective term for all policymaking officials of a government; the execution and implementation of public policy.
Microsoft	Microsoft is a multinational computer technology corporation with 2004 global annual sales of US$39.79 billion and 71,553 employees in 102 countries and regions as of July 2006. It develops, manufactures, licenses, and supports a wide range of software products for computing devices.
Small business	Small business refers to a business that is independently owned and operated, is not dominant in its field of operation, and meets certain standards of size in terms of employees or annual receipts.
Marketing	Promoting and selling products or services to customers, or prospective customers, is referred to as marketing.
Marketing research	Marketing research refers to the analysis of markets to determine opportunities and challenges, and to find the information needed to make good decisions.
Personnel	A collective term for all of the employees of an organization. Personnel is also commonly used to refer to the personnel management function or the organizational unit responsible for administering personnel programs.
Human resources	Human resources refers to the individuals within the firm, and to the portion of the firm's organization that deals with hiring, firing, training, and other personnel issues.
Budget	Budget refers to an account, usually for a year, of the planned expenditures and the expected receipts of an entity. For a government, the receipts are tax revenues.
Annuity	A contract to make regular payments to a person for life or for a fixed period is an annuity.
Bayer	Bayer is a German chemical and pharmaceutical company founded in 1863. By 1899, their trademark Aspirin was registered worldwide for the Bayer brand of acetylsalicylic acid, but through the widespread use to describe all brands of the compound, and Bayer's inability to protect its trademark the word "aspirin" lost its trademark status in the United States and some other countries.
Insurance	Insurance refers to a system by which individuals can reduce their exposure to risk of large losses by spreading the risks among a large number of persons.
Premium	Premium refers to the fee charged by an insurance company for an insurance policy. The rate of losses must be relatively predictable: In order to set the premium (prices) insurers must be able to estimate them accurately.

Draft	A signed, written order by which one party instructs another party to pay a specified sum to a third party, at sight or at a specific date is a draft.
Insurance	Insurance refers to a system by which individuals can reduce their exposure to risk of large losses by spreading the risks among a large number of persons.
Brief	Brief refers to a statement of a party's case or legal arguments, usually prepared by an attorney. Also used to make legal arguments before appellate courts.
Press release	A written public news announcement normally distributed to major news services is referred to as press release.
Ethical dilemma	An ethical dilemma is a situation that often involves an apparent conflict between moral imperatives, in which to obey one would result in transgressing another.
Infraction	Infraction is an essentially minor violation of law where the penalty upon conviction only consists of monetary forfeiture. A violation of law which could include imprisonment is a crime. It is distinguished from a misdemeanor or a felony in that the penalty for an infraction cannot include any imprisonment.
Supply	Supply is the aggregate amount of any material good that can be called into being at a certain price point; it comprises one half of the equation of supply and demand. In classical economic theory, a curve representing supply is one of the factors that produce price.
News release	A publicity tool consisting of an announcement regarding changes in the company or the product line is called a news release.
Publicity	Publicity refers to any information about an individual, product, or organization that's distributed to the public through the media and that's not paid for or controlled by the seller.
Public relations	Public relations refers to the management function that evaluates public attitudes, changes policies and procedures in response to the public's requests, and executes a program of action and information to earn public understanding and acceptance.
Trade show	A type of exhibition or forum where manufacturers can display their products to current as well as prospective buyers is referred to as trade show.
Service	Service refers to a "non tangible product" that is not embodied in a physical good and that typically effects some change in another product, person, or institution. Contrasts with good.
Discount	The difference between the face value of a bond and its selling price, when a bond is sold for less than its face value it's referred to as a discount.
Estate	An estate is the totality of the legal rights, interests, entitlements and obligations attaching to property. In the context of wills and probate, it refers to the totality of the property which the deceased owned or in which some interest was held.
Heir	In common law jurisdictions an heir is a person who is entitled to receive a share of the decedent's property via the rules of inheritance in the jurisdiction where the decedent died or owned property at the time of his death.
Trust	An arrangement in which shareholders of independent firms agree to give up their stock in exchange for trust certificates that entitle them to a share of the trust's common profits.
Fund	Independent accounting entity with a self-balancing set of accounts segregated for the purposes of carrying on specific activities is referred to as a fund.
Bond	Bond refers to a debt instrument, issued by a borrower and promising a specified stream of payments to the purchaser, usually regular interest payments plus a final repayment of

Go to **Cram101.com** for the Practice Tests for this Chapter.

principal.

Microsoft	Microsoft is a multinational computer technology corporation with 2004 global annual sales of US$39.79 billion and 71,553 employees in 102 countries and regions as of July 2006. It develops, manufactures, licenses, and supports a wide range of software products for computing devices.
Extension	Extension refers to an out-of-court settlement in which creditors agree to allow the firm more time to meet its financial obligations. A new repayment schedule will be developed, subject to the acceptance of creditors.
Vendor	A person who sells property to a vendee is a vendor. The words vendor and vendee are more commonly applied to the seller and purchaser of real estate, and the words seller and buyer are more commonly applied to the seller and purchaser of personal property.
Shelf life	Shelf life is the length of time that corresponds to a tolerable loss in quality of a processed food and other perishable items.
Users	Users refer to people in the organization who actually use the product or service purchased by the buying center.
Investment	Investment refers to spending for the production and accumulation of capital and additions to inventories. In a financial sense, buying an asset with the expectation of making a return.
Gain	In finance, gain is a profit or an increase in value of an investment such as a stock or bond. Gain is calculated by fair market value or the proceeds from the sale of the investment minus the sum of the purchase price and all costs associated with it.
Target audience	That group that composes the present and potential prospects for a product or service is called the target audience.
Security	Security refers to a claim on the borrower future income that is sold by the borrower to the lender. A security is a type of transferable interest representing financial value.
Customer service	The ability of logistics management to satisfy users in terms of time, dependability, communication, and convenience is called the customer service.
Holding	The holding is a court's determination of a matter of law based on the issue presented in the particular case. In other words: under this law, with these facts, this result.
Margin	A deposit by a buyer in stocks with a seller or a stockbroker, as security to cover fluctuations in the market in reference to stocks that the buyer has purchased but for which he has not paid is a margin. Commodities are also traded on margin.
Balance	In banking and accountancy, the outstanding balance is the amount of money owned, (or due), that remains in a deposit account (or a loan account) at a given date, after all past remittances, payments and withdrawal have been accounted for. It can be positive (then, in the balance sheet of a firm, it is an asset) or negative (a liability).
Budget	Budget refers to an account, usually for a year, of the planned expenditures and the expected receipts of an entity. For a government, the receipts are tax revenues.
Polaroid	The Polaroid Corporation was founded in 1937 by Edwin H. Land. It is most famous for its instant film cameras, which reached the market in 1948, and continue to be the company's flagship product line.
Preference	The act of a debtor in paying or securing one or more of his creditors in a manner more favorable to them than to other creditors or to the exclusion of such other creditors is a preference. In the absence of statute, a preference is perfectly good, but to be legal it must be bona fide, and not a mere subterfuge of the debtor to secure a future benefit to himself or to prevent the application of his property to his debts.

Technology	The body of knowledge and techniques that can be used to combine economic resources to produce goods and services is called technology.
Option	A contract that gives the purchaser the option to buy or sell the underlying financial instrument at a specified price, called the exercise price or strike price, within a specific period of time.
Layout	Layout refers to the physical arrangement of the various parts of an advertisement including the headline, subheads, illustrations, body copy, and any identifying marks.
Pica	Pica refers to the unit for measuring width in printing. There are 6 picas to an inch. A page of type 24 picas wide is 4 inches wide.
Effective communication	When the intended meaning equals the perceived meaning it is called effective communication.
Code of ethics	A formal statement of ethical principles and rules of conduct is a code of ethics. Some may have the force of law; these are often promulgated by the (quasi-)governmental agency responsible for licensing a profession. Violations of these codes may be subject to administrative (e.g., loss of license), civil or penal remedies.

Instrument	Instrument refers to an economic variable that is controlled by policy makers and can be used to influence other variables, called targets. Examples are monetary and fiscal policies used to achieve external and internal balance.
Press release	A written public news announcement normally distributed to major news services is referred to as press release.
Management	Management characterizes the process of leading and directing all or part of an organization, often a business, through the deployment and manipulation of resources. Early twentieth-century management writer Mary Parker Follett defined management as "the art of getting things done through people."
American Management Association	American Management Association International is the world's largest membership-based management development and executive training organization. Their products include instructor led seminars, workshops, conferences, customized corporate programs, online learning, books, newsletters, research surveys and reports.
Plagiarism	Plagiarism is a form of academic dishonesty, it is a matter of deceit: fooling a reader into believing that certain written material is original when it is not. Plagiarism is a serious academic offense when the goal is to obtain some sort of personal academic credit or personal recognition.
Mistake	In contract law a mistake is incorrect understanding by one or more parties to a contract and may be used as grounds to invalidate the agreement. Common law has identified three different types of mistake in contract: unilateral mistake, mutual mistake, and common mistake.
Credit	Credit refers to a recording as positive in the balance of payments, any transaction that gives rise to a payment into the country, such as an export, the sale of an asset, or borrowing from abroad.
Administration	Administration refers to the management and direction of the affairs of governments and institutions; a collective term for all policymaking officials of a government; the execution and implementation of public policy.
Budget	Budget refers to an account, usually for a year, of the planned expenditures and the expected receipts of an entity. For a government, the receipts are tax revenues.
Committee	A long-lasting, sometimes permanent team in the organization structure created to deal with tasks that recur regularly is the committee.
Personnel	A collective term for all of the employees of an organization. Personnel is also commonly used to refer to the personnel management function or the organizational unit responsible for administering personnel programs.
Accounting	A system that collects and processes financial information about an organization and reports that information to decision makers is referred to as accounting.
Service	Service refers to a "non tangible product" that is not embodied in a physical good and that typically effects some change in another product, person, or institution. Contrasts with good.
Corporation	A legal entity chartered by a state or the Federal government that is distinct and separate from the individuals who own it is a corporation. This separation gives the corporation unique powers which other legal entities lack.
Production	The creation of finished goods and services using the factors of production: land, labor, capital, entrepreneurship, and knowledge.
Operation	A standardized method or technique that is performed repetitively, often on different materials resulting in different finished goods is called an operation.

Insurance	Insurance refers to a system by which individuals can reduce their exposure to risk of large losses by spreading the risks among a large number of persons.
Draft	A signed, written order by which one party instructs another party to pay a specified sum to a third party, at sight or at a specific date is a draft.
Consultant	A professional that provides expert advice in a particular field or area in which customers occassionaly require this type of knowledge is a consultant.
Research report	A research report is a business report produced by business research firms by their financial analysts. They are designed to dig out the important pieces of companies operational and financial reporting to paint a picture of the future of companies to assist debt and equity investing.
Evaluation	The consumer's appraisal of the product or brand on important attributes is called evaluation.
Secondary research	Research or data that is already gathered by someone else for another purpose is called secondary research.
Verification	Verification refers to the final stage of the creative process where the validity or truthfulness of the insight is determined. The feedback portion of communication in which the receiver sends a message to the source indicating receipt of the message and the degree to which he or she understood the message.
Respondent	Respondent refers to a term often used to describe the party charged in an administrative proceeding. The party adverse to the appellant in a case appealed to a higher court.
Contract	A contract is a "promise" or an "agreement" that is enforced or recognized by the law. In the civil law, a contract is considered to be part of the general law of obligations.
Firm	An organization that employs resources to produce a good or service for profit and owns and operates one or more plants is referred to as a firm.
Brief	Brief refers to a statement of a party's case or legal arguments, usually prepared by an attorney. Also used to make legal arguments before appellate courts.
Scope	Scope of a project is the sum total of all projects products and their requirements or features.
Human resources	Human resources refers to the individuals within the firm, and to the portion of the firm's organization that deals with hiring, firing, training, and other personnel issues.
Margin	A deposit by a buyer in stocks with a seller or a stockbroker, as security to cover fluctuations in the market in reference to stocks that the buyer has purchased but for which he has not paid is a margin. Commodities are also traded on margin.
Industry	A group of firms that produce identical or similar products is an industry. It is also used specifically to refer to an area of economic production focused on manufacturing which involves large amounts of capital investment before any profit can be realized, also called "heavy industry".
Gain	In finance, gain is a profit or an increase in value of an investment such as a stock or bond. Gain is calculated by fair market value or the proceeds from the sale of the investment minus the sum of the purchase price and all costs associated with it.
Configuration	An organization's shape, which reflects the division of labor and the means of coordinating the divided tasks is configuration.
Commerce	Commerce is the exchange of something of value between two entities. It is the central mechanism from which capitalism is derived.

Go to **Cram101.com** for the Practice Tests for this Chapter.

Economic development	Increase in the economic standard of living of a country's population, normally accomplished by increasing its stocks of physical and human capital and improving its technology is an economic development.
Market	A market is, as defined in economics, a social arrangement that allows buyers and sellers to discover information and carry out a voluntary exchange of goods or services.
Brand	A name, symbol, or design that identifies the goods or services of one seller or group of sellers and distinguishes them from the goods and services of competitors is a brand.
Appreciation	Appreciation refers to a rise in the value of a country's currency on the exchange market, relative either to a particular other currency or to a weighted average of other currencies. The currency is said to appreciate. Opposite of 'depreciation.' Appreciation can also refer to the increase in value of any asset.
Technology	The body of knowledge and techniques that can be used to combine economic resources to produce goods and services is called technology.
Plea	A plea is an answer to a declaration or complaint or any material allegation of fact therein that, if untrue, would defeat the action. In criminal procedure, a plea is the matter that the accused, on his arraignment, alleges in answer to the charge against him.
Labor force	In economics the labor force is the group of people who have a potential for being employed.
Labor	People's physical and mental talents and efforts that are used to help produce goods and services are called labor.
Gap	In December of 1995, Gap became the first major North American retailer to accept independent monitoring of the working conditions in a contract factory producing its garments. Gap is the largest specialty retailer in the United States.
Business Week	Business Week is a business magazine published by McGraw-Hill. It was first published in 1929 under the direction of Malcolm Muir, who was serving as president of the McGraw-Hill Publishing company at the time. It is considered to be the standard both in industry and among students.
Objection	In the trial of a case the formal remonstrance made by counsel to something that has been said or done, in order to obtain the court's ruling thereon is an objection.
Staffing	Staffing refers to a management function that includes hiring, motivating, and retaining the best people available to accomplish the company's objectives.
Profit	Profit refers to the return to the resource entrepreneurial ability; total revenue minus total cost.
Manufacturing	Production of goods primarily by the application of labor and capital to raw materials and other intermediate inputs, in contrast to agriculture, mining, forestry, fishing, and services a manufacturing.
Assembly line	An assembly line is a manufacturing process in which interchangeable parts are added to a product in a sequential manner to create a finished product.
Inventory	Tangible property held for sale in the normal course of business or used in producing goods or services for sale is an inventory.
Operating budget	An operating budget is the annual budget of an activity stated in terms of Budget Classification Code, functional/subfunctional categories and cost accounts. It contains estimates of the total value of resources required for the performance of the operation including reimbursable work or services for others.
Interest	In finance and economics, interest is the price paid by a borrower for the use of a lender's

	money. In other words, interest is the amount of paid to "rent" money for a period of time.
Fund	Independent accounting entity with a self-balancing set of accounts segregated for the purposes of carrying on specific activities is referred to as a fund.
Investment	Investment refers to spending for the production and accumulation of capital and additions to inventories. In a financial sense, buying an asset with the expectation of making a return.
Security	Security refers to a claim on the borrower future income that is sold by the borrower to the lender. A security is a type of transferable interest representing financial value.
Assignment	A transfer of property or some right or interest is referred to as assignment.

Telecommuting	Telecommuting is a work arrangement in which employees enjoy limited flexibility in working location and hours.
Productivity	Productivity refers to the total output of goods and services in a given period of time divided by work hours.
Expense	In accounting, an expense represents an event in which an asset is used up or a liability is incurred. In terms of the accounting equation, expenses reduce owners' equity.
Technology	The body of knowledge and techniques that can be used to combine economic resources to produce goods and services is called technology.
Telecommute	To work at home and keep in touch with the company through telecommunications is referred to as telecommute.
Option	A contract that gives the purchaser the option to buy or sell the underlying financial instrument at a specified price, called the exercise price or strike price, within a specific period of time.
Organizational structure	Organizational structure is the way in which the interrelated groups of an organization are constructed. From a managerial point of view the main concerns are ensuring effective communication and coordination.
Small business	Small business refers to a business that is independently owned and operated, is not dominant in its field of operation, and meets certain standards of size in terms of employees or annual receipts.
Electronic mail	Electronic mail refers to electronic written communication between individuals using computers connected to the Internet.
Facilitator	A facilitator is someone who skilfully helps a group of people understand their common objectives and plan to achieve them without personally taking any side of the argument.
Preparation	Preparation refers to usually the first stage in the creative process. It includes education and formal training.
Board of directors	The group of individuals elected by the stockholders of a corporation to oversee its operations is a board of directors.
Distribution	Distribution in economics, the manner in which total output and income is distributed among individuals or factors.
Attachment	Attachment in general, the process of taking a person's property under an appropriate judicial order by an appropriate officer of the court. Used for a variety of purposes, including the acquisition of jurisdiction over the property seized and the securing of property that may be used to satisfy a debt.
Investment	Investment refers to spending for the production and accumulation of capital and additions to inventories. In a financial sense, buying an asset with the expectation of making a return.
Regular meeting	A meeting held by the board of directors that is held at regular intervals at the time and place established in the bylaws is called a regular meeting.
Policy	Similar to a script in that a policy can be a less than completely rational decision-making method. Involves the use of a pre-existing set of decision steps for any problem that presents itself.
Bylaw	In corporation law, a document that supplements the articles of incorporation and contains less important rights, powers, and responsibilities of a corporation and its shareholders, officers, and directors is referred to as a bylaw.
Budget	Budget refers to an account, usually for a year, of the planned expenditures and the expected

Go to **Cram101.com** for the Practice Tests for this Chapter.

receipts of an entity. For a government, the receipts are tax revenues.

Committee	A long-lasting, sometimes permanent team in the organization structure created to deal with tasks that recur regularly is the committee.
Indexing	Indexing refers to provisions in a law or a contract whereby monetary payments are automatically adjusted whenever a specified price index changes.
Action plan	Action plan refers to a written document that includes the steps the trainee and manager will take to ensure that training transfers to the job.
Points	Loan origination fees that may be deductible as interest by a buyer of property. A seller of property who pays points reduces the selling price by the amount of the points paid for the buyer.
Production	The creation of finished goods and services using the factors of production: land, labor, capital, entrepreneurship, and knowledge.
Vendor	A person who sells property to a vendee is a vendor. The words vendor and vendee are more commonly applied to the seller and purchaser of real estate, and the words seller and buyer are more commonly applied to the seller and purchaser of personal property.
Product line	A group of products that are physically similar or are intended for a similar market are called the product line.
Capital	Capital generally refers to financial wealth, especially that used to start or maintain a business. In classical economics, capital is one of four factors of production, the others being land and labor and entrepreneurship.
Margin	A deposit by a buyer in stocks with a seller or a stockbroker, as security to cover fluctuations in the market in reference to stocks that the buyer has purchased but for which he has not paid is a margin. Commodities are also traded on margin.
Stockholder	A stockholder is an individual or company (including a corporation) that legally owns one or more shares of stock in a joined stock company. The shareholders are the owners of a corporation. Companies listed at the stock market strive to enhance shareholder value.
Revenue	Revenue is a U.S. business term for the amount of money that a company receives from its activities, mostly from sales of products and/or services to customers.
Budget committee	A group of top-management personnel who advise the budget director during the preparation of the budget is a budget committee.
Regulation	Regulation refers to restrictions state and federal laws place on business with regard to the conduct of its activities.
Service	Service refers to a "non tangible product" that is not embodied in a physical good and that typically effects some change in another product, person, or institution. Contrasts with good.
Interest	In finance and economics, interest is the price paid by a borrower for the use of a lender's money. In other words, interest is the amount of paid to "rent" money for a period of time.
Management	Management characterizes the process of leading and directing all or part of an organization, often a business, through the deployment and manipulation of resources. Early twentieth-century management writer Mary Parker Follett defined management as "the art of getting things done through people."
Insurance	Insurance refers to a system by which individuals can reduce their exposure to risk of large losses by spreading the risks among a large number of persons.
Fringe benefit	Benefits such as sick-leave pay, vacation pay, pension plans, and health plans that represent

additional compenzation to employees beyond base wages is a fringe benefit.

Treasurer	In many governments, a treasurer is the person responsible for running the treasury. Treasurers are also employed by organizations to look after funds.
Public relations	Public relations refers to the management function that evaluates public attitudes, changes policies and procedures in response to the public's requests, and executes a program of action and information to earn public understanding and acceptance.
Specialist	A specialist is a trader who makes a market in one or several stocks and holds the limit order book for those stocks.
Executive Council	An Executive Council in Commonwealth constitutional practice based on the Westminster system exercises executive power and is the top tier of a government led by a Governor-General, Governor, Lieutenant-Governor or Administrator (all "governors").
Audit	An examination of the financial reports to ensure that they represent what they claim and conform with generally accepted accounting principles is referred to as audit.

Productivity	Productivity refers to the total output of goods and services in a given period of time divided by work hours.
Marketing	Promoting and selling products or services to customers, or prospective customers, is referred to as marketing.
Interest	In finance and economics, interest is the price paid by a borrower for the use of a lender's money. In other words, interest is the amount of paid to "rent" money for a period of time.
Inventory	Tangible property held for sale in the normal course of business or used in producing goods or services for sale is an inventory.
Foundation	A Foundation is a type of philanthropic organization set up by either individuals or institutions as a legal entity (either as a corporation or trust) with the purpose of distributing grants to support causes in line with the goals of the foundation.
Aptitude	An aptitude is an innate inborn ability to do a certain kind of work. Aptitudes may be physical or mental. Many of them have been identified and are testable.
Appeal	Appeal refers to the act of asking an appellate court to overturn a decision after the trial court's final judgment has been entered.
Freelance	A freelance worker is a self-employed person working in a profession or trade in which full-time employment is also common.
Gain	In finance, gain is a profit or an increase in value of an investment such as a stock or bond. Gain is calculated by fair market value or the proceeds from the sale of the investment minus the sum of the purchase price and all costs associated with it.
Service	Service refers to a "non tangible product" that is not embodied in a physical good and that typically effects some change in another product, person, or institution. Contrasts with good.
Preparation	Preparation refers to usually the first stage in the creative process. It includes education and formal training.
Balance	In banking and accountancy, the outstanding balance is the amount of money owned, (or due), that remains in a deposit account (or a loan account) at a given date, after all past remittances, payments and withdrawal have been accounted for. It can be positive (then, in the balance sheet of a firm, it is an asset) or negative (a liability).
Affiliates	Local television stations that are associated with a major network are called affiliates. Affiliates agree to preempt time during specified hours for programming provided by the network and carry the advertising contained in the program.
Advertisement	Advertisement is the promotion of goods, services, companies and ideas, usually by an identified sponsor. Marketers see advertising as part of an overall promotional strategy.
Industry	A group of firms that produce identical or similar products is an industry. It is also used specifically to refer to an area of economic production focused on manufacturing which involves large amounts of capital investment before any profit can be realized, also called "heavy industry".
Contract	A contract is a "promise" or an "agreement" that is enforced or recognized by the law. In the civil law, a contract is considered to be part of the general law of obligations.
Telecommuting	Telecommuting is a work arrangement in which employees enjoy limited flexibility in working location and hours.
Brief	Brief refers to a statement of a party's case or legal arguments, usually prepared by an attorney. Also used to make legal arguments before appellate courts.

Go to **Cram101.com** for the Practice Tests for this Chapter.

Management	Management characterizes the process of leading and directing all or part of an organization, often a business, through the deployment and manipulation of resources. Early twentieth-century management writer Mary Parker Follett defined management as "the art of getting things done through people."
Accounting	A system that collects and processes financial information about an organization and reports that information to decision makers is referred to as accounting.
Manufacturing	Production of goods primarily by the application of labor and capital to raw materials and other intermediate inputs, in contrast to agriculture, mining, forestry, fishing, and services a manufacturing.
Firm	An organization that employs resources to produce a good or service for profit and owns and operates one or more plants is referred to as a firm.
Bookkeeping	The recording of business transactions is called bookkeeping.
Supply	Supply is the aggregate amount of any material good that can be called into being at a certain price point; it comprises one half of the equation of supply and demand. In classical economic theory, a curve representing supply is one of the factors that produce price.
Applicant	In many tribunal and administrative law suits, the person who initiates the claim is called the applicant.
Administration	Administration refers to the management and direction of the affairs of governments and institutions; a collective term for all policymaking officials of a government; the execution and implementation of public policy.
Capital	Capital generally refers to financial wealth, especially that used to start or maintain a business. In classical economics, capital is one of four factors of production, the others being land and labor and entrepreneurship.
Fund	Independent accounting entity with a self-balancing set of accounts segregated for the purposes of carrying on specific activities is referred to as a fund.
Press release	A written public news announcement normally distributed to major news services is referred to as press release.
Promotion	Promotion refers to all the techniques sellers use to motivate people to buy products or services. An attempt by marketers to inform people about products and to persuade them to participate in an exchange.
Advertising	Advertising refers to paid, nonpersonal communication through various media by organizations and individuals who are in some way identified in the advertising message.
Layout	Layout refers to the physical arrangement of the various parts of an advertisement including the headline, subheads, illustrations, body copy, and any identifying marks.
Microsoft	Microsoft is a multinational computer technology corporation with 2004 global annual sales of US$39.79 billion and 71,553 employees in 102 countries and regions as of July 2006. It develops, manufactures, licenses, and supports a wide range of software products for computing devices.
Shill	A shill is an associate of a person selling goods or services, who pretends no association to the seller and assumes the air of an enthusiastic customer.
Gap	In December of 1995, Gap became the first major North American retailer to accept independent monitoring of the working conditions in a contract factory producing its garments. Gap is the largest specialty retailer in the United States.
Graduation	Termination of a country's eligibility for GSP tariff preferences on the grounds that it has

progressed sufficiently, in terms of per capita income or another measure, that it is no longer in need to special and differential treatment is graduation.

Specialist	A specialist is a trader who makes a market in one or several stocks and holds the limit order book for those stocks.
Insurance	Insurance refers to a system by which individuals can reduce their exposure to risk of large losses by spreading the risks among a large number of persons.
Retail sale	The sale of goods and services to consumers for their own use is a retail sale.
Contribution	In business organization law, the cash or property contributed to a business by its owners is referred to as contribution.
Evaluation	The consumer's appraisal of the product or brand on important attributes is called evaluation.
Technology	The body of knowledge and techniques that can be used to combine economic resources to produce goods and services is called technology.
Matching	Matching refers to an accounting concept that establishes when expenses are recognized. Expenses are matched with the revenues they helped to generate and are recognized when those revenues are recognized.
Points	Loan origination fees that may be deductible as interest by a buyer of property. A seller of property who pays points reduces the selling price by the amount of the points paid for the buyer.
Receiver	A person that is appointed as a custodian of other people's property by a court of law or a creditor of the owner, pending a lawsuit or reorganization is called a receiver.
Confirmed	When the seller's bank agrees to assume liability on the letter of credit issued by the buyer's bank the transaction is confirmed. The term means that the credit is not only backed up by the issuing foreign bank, but that payment is also guaranteed by the notifying American bank.
Personnel	A collective term for all of the employees of an organization. Personnel is also commonly used to refer to the personnel management function or the organizational unit responsible for administering personnel programs.
Human resources	Human resources refers to the individuals within the firm, and to the portion of the firm's organization that deals with hiring, firing, training, and other personnel issues.
Annual report	An annual report is prepared by corporate management that presents financial information including financial statements, footnotes, and the management discussion and analysis.
Portfolio	In finance, a portfolio is a collection of investments held by an institution or a private individual. Holding but not always a portfolio is part of an investment and risk-limiting strategy called diversification. By owning several assets, certain types of risk (in particular specific risk) can be reduced.
Tangible	Having a physical existence is referred to as the tangible. Personal property other than real estate, such as cars, boats, stocks, or other assets.
Binder	Binder, also called a binding slip, refers to a brief memorandum or agreement issued by an insurer as a temporary policy for the convenience of all the parties, constituting a present insurance in the amount specified, to continue in force until the execution of a formal policy.
Assessment	Collecting information and providing feedback to employees about their behavior, communication style, or skills is an assessment.

Sales promotion	Sales promotion refers to the promotional tool that stimulates consumer purchasing and dealer interest by means of short-term activities.
Attest	To bear witness to is called attest. To affirm, certify by oath or signature. It is an official act establishing authenticity.
Asset	An item of property, such as land, capital, money, a share in ownership, or a claim on others for future payment, such as a bond or a bank deposit is an asset.

Portfolio	In finance, a portfolio is a collection of investments held by an institution or a private individual. Holding but not always a portfolio is part of an investment and risk-limiting strategy called diversification. By owning several assets, certain types of risk (in particular specific risk) can be reduced.
Inventory	Tangible property held for sale in the normal course of business or used in producing goods or services for sale is an inventory.
Trust	An arrangement in which shareholders of independent firms agree to give up their stock in exchange for trust certificates that entitle them to a share of the trust's common profits.
Marketing	Promoting and selling products or services to customers, or prospective customers, is referred to as marketing.
Interest	In finance and economics, interest is the price paid by a borrower for the use of a lender's money. In other words, interest is the amount of paid to "rent" money for a period of time.
Authority	Authority in agency law, refers to an agent's ability to affect his principal's legal relations with third parties. Also used to refer to an actor's legal power or ability to do something. In addition, sometimes used to refer to a statute, case, or other legal source that justifies a particular result.
Receiver	A person that is appointed as a custodian of other people's property by a court of law or a creditor of the owner, pending a lawsuit or reorganization is called a receiver.
Service	Service refers to a "non tangible product" that is not embodied in a physical good and that typically effects some change in another product, person, or institution. Contrasts with good.
Advertisement	Advertisement is the promotion of goods, services, companies and ideas, usually by an identified sponsor. Marketers see advertising as part of an overall promotional strategy.
Competitor	Other organizations in the same industry or type of business that provide a good or service to the same set of customers is referred to as a competitor.
Applicant	In many tribunal and administrative law suits, the person who initiates the claim is called the applicant.
Accounting	A system that collects and processes financial information about an organization and reports that information to decision makers is referred to as accounting.
Lease	A contract for the possession and use of land or other property, including goods, on one side, and a recompense of rent or other income on the other is the lease.
Accounting method	Accounting method refers to the method under which income and expenses are determined for tax purposes. Important accounting methods include the cash basis and the accrual basis.
Financial report	Financial report refers to a written statement-also called an accountant's certificate, accountant's opinion, or audit report-prepared by an independent accountant or auditor after an audit.
Policy	Similar to a script in that a policy can be a less than completely rational decision-making method. Involves the use of a pre-existing set of decision steps for any problem that presents itself.
Retailing	All activities involved in selling, renting, and providing goods and services to ultimate consumers for personal, family, or household use is referred to as retailing.
Human resources	Human resources refers to the individuals within the firm, and to the portion of the firm's organization that deals with hiring, firing, training, and other personnel issues.
Advertising	Advertising refers to paid, nonpersonal communication through various media by organizations

Go to **Cram101.com** for the Practice Tests for this Chapter.

and individuals who are in some way identified in the advertising message.

Merchant	Under the Uniform Commercial Code, one who regularly deals in goods of the kind sold in the contract at issue, or holds himself out as having special knowledge or skill relevant to such goods, or who makes the sale through an agent who regularly deals in such goods or claims such knowledge or skill is referred to as merchant.
Closing	The finalization of a real estate sales transaction that passes title to the property from the seller to the buyer is referred to as a closing. Closing is a sales term which refers to the process of making a sale. It refers to reaching the final step, which may be an exchange of money or acquiring a signature.
Bond	Bond refers to a debt instrument, issued by a borrower and promising a specified stream of payments to the purchaser, usually regular interest payments plus a final repayment of principal.
Exchange	The trade of things of value between buyer and seller so that each is better off after the trade is called the exchange.
Preparation	Preparation refers to usually the first stage in the creative process. It includes education and formal training.
Annual report	An annual report is prepared by corporate management that presents financial information including financial statements, footnotes, and the management discussion and analysis.
Corporation	A legal entity chartered by a state or the Federal government that is distinct and separate from the individuals who own it is a corporation. This separation gives the corporation unique powers which other legal entities lack.
Complement	A good that is used in conjunction with another good is a complement. For example, cameras and film would complement eachother.
Personnel	A collective term for all of the employees of an organization. Personnel is also commonly used to refer to the personnel management function or the organizational unit responsible for administering personnel programs.
Screening	Screening in economics refers to a strategy of combating adverse selection, one of the potential decision-making complications in cases of asymmetric information.
Brief	Brief refers to a statement of a party's case or legal arguments, usually prepared by an attorney. Also used to make legal arguments before appellate courts.
Comprehensive	A comprehensive refers to a layout accurate in size, color, scheme, and other necessary details to show how a final ad will look. For presentation only, never for reproduction.
Customs	Customs is an authority or agency in a country responsible for collecting customs duties and for controlling the flow of people, animals and goods (including personal effects and hazardous items) in and out of the country.
Supervisor	A Supervisor is an employee of an organization with some of the powers and responsibilities of management, occupying a role between true manager and a regular employee. A Supervisor position is typically the first step towards being promoted into a management role.
Market	A market is, as defined in economics, a social arrangement that allows buyers and sellers to discover information and carry out a voluntary exchange of goods or services.
Points	Loan origination fees that may be deductible as interest by a buyer of property. A seller of property who pays points reduces the selling price by the amount of the points paid for the buyer.
Consideration	Consideration in contract law, a basic requirement for an enforceable agreement under

	traditional contract principles, defined in this text as legal value, bargained for and given in exchange for an act or promise. In corporation law, cash or property contributed to a corporation in exchange for shares, or a promise to contribute such cash or property.
Quick response	An inventory management system designed to reduce the retailer's lead-time, thereby lowering its inventory investment, improving customer service levels, and reducing logistics expense is referred to as quick response.
Specialist	A specialist is a trader who makes a market in one or several stocks and holds the limit order book for those stocks.
Graduation	Termination of a country's eligibility for GSP tariff preferences on the grounds that it has progressed sufficiently, in terms of per capita income or another measure, that it is no longer in need to special and differential treatment is graduation.
Goodwill	Goodwill is an important accounting concept that describes the value of a business entity not directly attributable to its tangible assets and liabilities.
Chief executive officer	A chief executive officer is the highest-ranking corporate officer or executive officer of a corporation, or agency. In closely held corporations, it is general business culture that the office chief executive officer is also the chairman of the board.
Transcript	A copy of writing is referred to as a transcript. It is the official record of proceedings in a trial or hearing.
Bottom line	The bottom line is net income on the last line of a income statement.

Printed in the United Kingdom
by Lightning Source UK Ltd.
119245UK00001B/129-130